Nature in the West Country

Other books by S. A. Manning

BROADLAND NATURALIST
The Soman-Wherry Press

THE RIGHT WAY TO UNDERSTAND THE COUNTRYSIDE
Right Way Books (Andrew George Elliot)

BAKERS AND BREAD
Basil Blackwell

TREES AND FORESTS
Basil Blackwell

THE LADYBIRD BOOK OF BUTTERFLIES, MOTHS AND OTHER INSECTS
Wills & Hepworth

SYSTEMATIC GUIDE TO FLOWERING PLANTS OF THE WORLD
Museum Press

THE INSECT WORLD
World's Work

THE WOODLAND WORLD
World's Work

THE NATURALIST IN SOUTH-EAST ENGLAND
(Kent, Surrey and Sussex)
David & Charles

NATURE IN EAST ANGLIA (Norfolk and Suffolk)
World's Work

PORTRAIT OF ESSEX
Robert Hale

PORTRAIT OF CAMBRIDGESHIRE
Robert Hale

S. A. Manning, F.L.S.

Nature in the West Country

Somerset, Devon and Cornwall

WORLD'S WORK LTD
The Windmill Press Kingswood Tadworth Surrey

TO THE READER

The author hopes that, if you are not already a member, you will join the nature conservation trust caring for the county in which you live or spend your holidays. It needs *your* support!

Trying hard to practise what he preaches, he is a life member of each of the West Country trusts, whose addresses are:

Cornwall Naturalists' Trust,
Trendrine, Zennor, St Ives, Cornwall, TR26 3BW.
Devon Trust for Nature Conservation,
75 Queen Street, Exeter, Devon, EX4 3RX.
Somerset Trust for Nature Conservation,
Fyne Court, Broomfield, Bridgwater, Somerset, TA5 2EQ.

ACKNOWLEDGEMENTS

The author and publisher are indebted to the following for permission to use their photographs.

THE WEST COUNTRY: SUB-REGIONS AND RESERVES
Nature Conservancy Council photographs on pages 11 and 23
Leonard and Marjorie Gayton all other photographs

MAMMALS
Geoffrey Kinns

BREEDING BIRDS
G. H. E. Young

AMPHIBIANS AND REPTILES
Geoffrey Kinns

BUTTERFLIES
J. B. and S. Bottomley

TREES, SHRUBS AND SOME OTHER PLANTS
Dr M. C. F. Proctor

Thanks are also due to Reginald and Marjorie Piggot who drew the maps.

Printed in Great Britain by
Fletcher & Son Ltd, Norwich
Hard cover edition SBN 437 09501 0
Paperback edition SBN 437 09502 9

To my fellow members
of the nature conservation trusts
for Somerset, Devon and Cornwall,
in the hope that we are joined
by many readers of this book.

Contents

Burrington Combe. Many trees, shrubs and smaller plants thrive here on limestone soils.

The West Country: sub-regions and reserves

The West Country holds a great wealth of interest for naturalists who experience something of it immediately on entering Somerset. Here the Mendips, steep-sided and flat-topped, form a compact line of hills, a Carboniferous Limestone mass. Thinly-covered slopes, cliffs and rock-ledges where lime-loving plants thrive, wooded slopes and higher ground whose acid soils are favoured by lime-avoiding plants are among the many habitats of this delightful district.

Cheddar Gorge, its mighty cliffs enlivened by contrasting and changing patterns of vegetation and flowers, is thronged with tourists in summer and should therefore be visited out of season or in early morning or late evening. The same applies to Burrington Combe, a popular place that is sometimes regarded as 'a miniature Cheddar Gorge', whose slopes and cliffs support yew, whitebeam, ash and many smaller lime-loving species.

Nature reserves and trails set up by the National Trust and other bodies enable one to escape the crowd and enjoy closer contact with wild things. Many of them will be mentioned in the text, but fuller details are given in the section *Reserves and other places to visit* towards the end of this book.

At Black Rock Nature Reserve, off the Cheddar Gorge road, the Somerset Trust for Nature Conservation (STNC) hopes to show that land similar to that at this National Trust property, with its plantations, woodland, rough grazing and scree (slopes of loose rock), can be managed in the combined interest of wildlife, agriculture, forestry and the general public. A marked nature trail takes visitors below one of many rock outcrops and through plantation and woodland. From one stop there is a panoramic view whose interesting features include Black Down, the much-visited highest point (1,067 ft) of the Mendip Hills, where fires have caused so much damage that breaks are being cut and maintained in the hope of containing future outbreaks.

Black Rock Gate on the Cheddar Gorge road also gives access to Velvet Bottom Nature Reserve where STNC work parties have cut fire-breaks across the valley and planted young hardwood trees on the slopes. Noted for its butterflies and other insects, this 42-acre reserve was established as the result of cooperation between STNC and Bristol Waterworks Company. Similar agreement between these bodies resulted in Long Wood, 42 acres off the Cheddar Gorge road past Black Rock, being managed as a nature reserve where a nature trail was established to mark European Conservation Year 1970. Visitors to this and many other West Country reserves are struck by the abundance of lichens, plants inside which two organisms, a fungus and an alga, live in a special kind of partnership.

Two miles south-east of Cheddar, Rodney Stoke National Nature Reserve includes 64 acres of woodland consisting mainly of ash, a characteristic tree of calcareous soils. Ash is also an important element in woodland at Ebbor Gorge National Nature Reserve, a National Trust property managed by the Nature Conservancy Council. Like other Mendip reserves, this wooded limestone gorge two miles north-west of Wells includes caves and other evidence of the dissolving action of rainwater on limestone. The display centre at the entrance to the car park illustrates the local geology and wildlife and should certainly be visited.

The Mendips extend westwards to the coast where, two miles south-west of Weston-super-Mare, Brean Down, the southern arm of Weston Bay, is a Site of Special Scientific Interest (SSSI). Out at sea, some three and a half miles from the tip of Brean Down, Steep Holm represents a former extension of the Mendip ridge. Brean Down and Steep Holm are discussed in later sections of this chapter.

Between the Mendips and the Quantocks much of the Somerset plain is occupied by the peaty and alluvial flats of the Somerset Levels, a 169,000-acre marshland area once described as a series of shallow saucers bounded by hills and coast. Improved permanent grass covers most of the Levels where farming, typically in small units devoted to dairying and the raising of beef cattle from the dairy herd, is assisted by a well-organized system of field drains, ditches, rhynes (the main flanking ditches), rivers and wide man-made channels. These waterways form habitats of animals and plants, and flooding, to which parts of the Levels are still subject on occasion, helps to encourage many kinds of birds.

These, like other elements of the fauna and flora, are increasingly subject to changing patterns of land use on the Levels. Major land drainage poses one considerable threat and, according to the Agricultural Advisory Council, about three-quarters of the total area could be made dry enough for highly productive arable cultivation. The modern peat-winning industry, with its huge excavations, has created another considerable threat, the development of mechanical methods having enabled peat, now extensively used in gardening and horticulture, to be extracted much more quickly and thoroughly than ever before.

The problems facing wildlife conservation on the Somerset Levels were examined by the Somerset Wetlands Project Group, a body representing all the various interests concerned, which was established as part of the Council of Europe's 1976/77 'Save Europe's Wetlands' campaign. In a consultation paper (1977), the group stated that if the present trends in agriculture and peat extraction continued, it seemed inevitable that extensive deterioration of the wildlife environment would follow. One of five options advanced to guide further action suggested a land-use strategy under which areas could be designated primarily for agriculture, peat winning or conservation. Several organizations, including the Nature Conservancy Council, have called for such a course of action, and no doubt the proposal will stimulate discussion.

Meanwhile a few areas have been established as nature reserves. Shapwick Heath, four miles west of Glastonbury, has the status of National Nature Reserve. Planning permission for the extraction of peat on 498 acres was, however, given in 1949, with no conditions attached. The Nature Conservancy Council holds the remaining 48 acres under a Nature Reserve Agreement in perpetuity. The 32-acre STNC reserve at Westhay Moor, between Glastonbury and Wedmore, includes old peat workings, deep cuttings containing water and sphagnum moss. Considerable efforts have been made to remove invading trees and scrub which would otherwise shade out smaller plants and also help to dry out the area. At Catcott Heath, a smaller STNC reserve in the same region, methods of controlling the growth of bog myrtle are being investigated, open water and open peat surfaces have been introduced to add to the variety of habitats, and ground is being prepared to receive species from areas where destruction awaits them. At Street Heath, a reserve set up by the local authority, the STNC is managing 21 acres of old peat workings, the habitat

Shapwick Heath National Nature Reserve,
where wildlife is being affected by the extraction of peat, stacks of which are seen in the foreground.

of bog asphodel, small bladderwort, least bur-reed and other noteworthy species.

The STNC, in its praiseworthy concern for the wildlife interests of this part of Somerset, has not only carried out an ecological survey of the Levels but it has also shown great interest in the 'brick pits' of the Sedgemoor area. Water filled these disused clay-pits, relics of the brick- and tile-making industry, and the growth of reeds and other vegetation attracted mallard, coot, sedge and reed warblers and other birds. Many pits have been filled in and others are subject to disturbance but some remain as refuges for wildlife. Once a private nature reserve, one area of clay-pits near Bridgwater has been established by the local authority as Screech Owl Local Nature Reserve.

Rising above the Somerset plain, the Quantock Hills stretch inland for about twelve miles from the A39 (Williton–Holford) road. An Area of Outstanding Natural Beauty, they reach a height of 1,261 ft at Wills Neck. Habitats include heaths, which suffer from accidental fires and the intrusion of vehicles, wooded combes, plantations and farmland where hedgerows are being removed. Several places in the Quantocks are open to naturalists. The National Trust safeguards 61 acres of open healthland at Longstone Hill, just west of Holford, and another $77\frac{1}{2}$ acres of woodland and heathland at its adjoining property,

Dunkery Beacon, the highest point of Exmoor, as seen from Lucott Moor.

The rich land of the Vale of Porlock stretches towards the sea.

Willoughby Cleeve. In the same area the Trust owns Shervage Wood, 136 acres of oak woodland and coppice and heathland. The two-and-a-half-mile Quantock Forest Trail from Seven Wells Bridge or Ramscombe Picnic Place takes visitors through Forestry Commission woods of coniferous and broad-leaved species, and there are walks through mixed woodland at Fyne Court, Broomfield, where the STNC has its headquarters and interpretation centre.

Geologically the Quantock Hills are regarded as a detached mass of Exmoor, and it is therefore appropriate that this last-named region, one with so many claims on the naturalist's attention, should now be considered. With its highest point at Dunkery Beacon (1,704 ft), Exmoor is, in very simple terms, a high plateau from which deeply-cut valleys carry swift-flowing streams. Administered as a National Park, Exmoor lies partly in Somerset (about 180 square miles), the rest being in Devon (about 85 square miles). About 17,000 acres (10 per cent of the total area) is woodland and 43,000 acres open moorland. The remaining 110,000 acres is largely devoted to grassland for sheep, cattle and ponies, though arable farming is carried on in certain areas, particularly on the rich land of the Vale of Porlock. Exmoor is almost entirely privately owned (roughly 86 per cent), but owners of open moorland are usually very tolerant of careful and considerate visitors and there are many waymarked walks.

Naturalists may gain access to many Exmoor habitats—heather moors, grass moors, bogs, woodland, plantations included, by visiting properties owned by the Somerset County Council, National Trust and Forestry Commission, carefully observing any restrictions which may be in force. In the north-west segment of the old Royal Forest of Exmoor the Somerset County Council owns some 2,000 acres on and around the high plateau of The Chains, a tussocky and

Burrator Lake, Dartmoor, where several types of wildfowl and waders are seen. The granite boulders (foreground) are the habitat of lichens.

boggy wilderness of particularly heavy rainfall whose highest point is at Chains Barrow (1,599 ft). In the late 1950s the Forestry Commission proposed to afforest The Chains. Considerable opposition was aroused and this led not only to the proposal being dropped but to the formation of the Exmoor Society as the Exmoor Branch of the Council for the Protection of Rural England (CPRE). As a watchdog intent on conserving the special character of Exmoor, the society is a vital force in the region.

Well to the east of The Chains the National Trust holds 12,420 acres, including 6,720 acres of the Moor and its highest point, Dunkery Beacon. Just to the north of this wonderful viewpoint is Cloutsham Nature Trail whose three-mile course is carefully signposted and marked. Starting from, and returning to, Webber's Post Car Park, the trail follows woodland, stream, farmland and dry scree slopes, passing on the way a wet muddy patch used by red deer for wallowing. South of Dunkery the National Trust has in Winsford Hill, a large stretch of open heather moor, another property where naturalists of all types will find plenty to interest them.

East of the Dunster–Dulverton road the Brendon Hills form a region that is largely separated from the main mass of Exmoor National Park by the deep valleys of the rivers Exe and Avill. Here much land has been reclaimed for farming and forestry. Some open moorland remains on the hill-tops and even Forestry Commission property often includes areas that are less 'regimented' than the plantations themselves. Entry to the forests is permitted in many places, there being, for example, a forest walk or trail at Chargot Wood.

STNC reserves not already mentioned include Chantry Lake and Woods, a wildlife refuge close to large limestone quarries near Mells, Frome and Asham Wood between Shepton Mallet and Frome, where coppicing (cutting back) of hazel has already admitted light and thus encouraged woodland plants to produce abundant flowers. Great Breach Wood, a 156-acre woodland reserve between Street and Somerton, has numerous oaks and other broad-leaved trees and is rich in butterflies. A magnificent gift to the STNC, it is the scene of scrub clearance and other hard work by enthusiastic volunteers. Such helpers, whose efforts are of the utmost value, have also worked at Dommett Wood, a beechwood reserve near Buckland St Mary, Chard. There are in Somerset many other places of interest to naturalists. Some of them are listed in the section *Reserves and other places to visit*.

Venturing deeper into the West Country, we reach Devon, like its neighbours an important centre of dairy farming. Here nature conservation is largely in the

View from Brown Willy, the highest point of Bodmin Moor. As on Dartmoor, the rocks are lichen-encrusted.

capable hands of the Nature Conservancy Council, the National Trust and the Devon Trust for Nature Conservation, though, as in so many other places, the Forestry Commission also plays a vital part by opening forest walks and by providing other facilities. Here again there is a great variety of scene and habitat.

There is some magnificent countryside in the Dartmoor National Park whose 365 square miles are devoted to stock-rearing, forestry, military use and other purposes, and include high moorland, granite tors, woodland and farmland, bogs, streams and steep-sided valleys.

On Dartmoor the Nature Conservancy Council protects three National and two Forest Nature Reserves and keeps an eye on a number of SSSIs, most of which are safeguarded by private owners. Two of the National Nature Reserves, Bovey Valley Woodlands and Yarner Wood, are near the eastern edge of the moor. Oak is the dominant tree in these native deciduous woodlands whose damper parts are particularly rich in mosses, lichens and liverworts. The third National Nature Reserve, Dendles Wood, is in the extreme south of the National Park. Oak is dominant in this reserve's western parts, which have been invaded by seedlings produced by beech planted in the eastern parts. The two Forest Nature Reserves, Black Tor Copse in the north-west corner of the National Park, and Wistman's Wood, a reserve nearer the centre of the moor, are small exposed woods where gnarled and stunted oaks grow between vast granite blocks, supporting on their trunks and branches luxuriant growths of ferns, mosses and lichens.

Some 4,000 acres of the High Moor are managed by the Forestry Commission whose main concern is, of course, producing the softwood timbers that are in such great demand commercially. By following either of the marked trails in Bellever Forest, one of the Commission's woods south of Postbridge, one sees not only Sitka spruce, Norway spruce, Contorta pine and other coniferous trees, but also alder, a species planted in wet areas, and other broad-leaved trees, and on forest rides ('roads') and stretches of unplanted moorland such examples of the natural vegetation as purple moor grass, heather and whortleberry. The land here rises up to Bellever Tor, a conical hill renowned for its symmetry and grace, whose summit rocks (1,456 ft) are the habitat of lichens that flourish in this exposed area of high rainfall.

Other Forestry Commission woods on Dartmoor are listed in the section *Reserves and other places to visit*, as are properties of the National Trust, which safeguards some 4,500 acres in the National Park. More than half of this acreage is occupied by Hentor and Willings Walls Warrens, open moorland rising to 1,600 ft in the south-west of the National Park. A marked trail on the adjoining National Trust property, Trowlesworthy Warren, passes by china-clay and old mineral workings, rough pasture and open moorland, small streams and boggy places, and takes the visitor to the top of Little Trowlesworthy Tor with its wide views across moorland and hill farmland.

Several reserves of the Devon Trust for Nature Conservation (DTNC) are situated along the eastern side of Dartmoor National Park. Moorland, valley woodland, riverside marsh and valley bog habitats are all represented in the largest of them, the 900-acre Dart Valley SSSI. The other DTNC Dartmoor reserves, though smaller, are equally valuable refuges for wildlife.

View from Hookney Tor on Dartmoor.

Ever since 1883 the Dartmoor Preservation Association has acted as watchdog, seeking, among other things, to protect the characteristic wildness, natural beauty and general scientific interest of Dartmoor. It has persistently called attention to the damaging and disturbing effects of activities as diverse as military training, quarrying and the winning and working of china clay. About ten years ago it bought High House Moor, part of which is classified as SSSI, thus saving from commercial afforestation some 142 acres of open moorland bordered by valley oakwoods.

Descending from Dartmoor's granite uplands but remaining inland (the coast is the subject of a later section of this chapter), visitors discover that much of Devon is devoted to crop, dairy and mixed farming and forestry. Fortunately for naturalists nature reserves and other protected areas have been set aside among the woods and pastures, hills and dales, of this fertile region. A few examples will show how various bodies have provided such cases.

In North Devon, Eggesford Forest, covering some 3,000 acres of the Taw valley, is not only a centre of timber production but also a reserve for many forms of wildlife. Two marked forest walks have been established here by the Forestry Commission who have collaborated with the DTNC in the preparation of detailed notes for visitors. Mature plantations and wet places are among the habitats in an area where steeper slopes and humid valley bottoms are devoted to forestry and better drained higher land to farming. In Holsworthy Woods, a stretch of Forestry Commission woodland about one and a half miles south of Holsworthy, a forest walk takes visitors among spruce, larch and pine growing in a heavy clay soil.

Below Wolborough Hill, in South Devon, the DTNC safeguards a small area of fen and reedbed, while at Chudleigh Knighton Heath it manages a 180-acre SSSI where its members have worked hard at clearing scrub and cutting fire-breaks. In East Devon the DTNC has at Hemyock two small reserves, Ashculm Turbary, with wet heath, bog and birch scrub, and Lickham Common whose 10 acres include both wet and drier places. In this part of Devon there is, as in so many other areas, access to Forestry Commission woods, the forest trail among both broad-leaved trees and conifers at Stoke Woods (part of Exeter Forest) being particularly well worth following.

One cannot leave East Devon without recalling that there its purchase of the waterway for recreational use enabled Devon County Council to set aside the Fossend Bridge–Lowdswell section of the Grand Western Canal as a nature reserve, though the entire stretch between Tiverton and Lowdswell is, in effect, a twelve-mile linear wildlife reserve. As if the wilderness of Dartmoor is not enough, West Devon has, among its other areas of interest to naturalists, Abbeyford Woods, north of Okehampton, and Plym Bridge Woods, not far from Plymouth.

Crossing into Cornwall, one passes through or close to the major granite mass of Bodmin Moor whose open uplands rise towards the county's highest hills, Brown Willy (1,375 ft) and Rough Tor. Apart from that of the Lizard Peninsula which, as we shall see, is in a special category, Bodmin Moor is the most south-westerly moorland of any size in Britain. There is no National Nature Reserve there but the Nature Conservancy Council has declared an area of

Many wild flowers grow on the sheltered banks of Cornish lanes like this one near Camelford.

The Great Hangman, between Combe Martin and Heddon's Mouth, a National Trust property to which there is access by coastal footpath.

some 6,200 acres a SSSI. The surface of the Moor, long grazed by cattle, sheep and ponies, is interrupted by bogs and pools and, rising to command fine views, granite tors whose lichen-encrusted rocks are exposed and windswept. At one such high-point, Rough Tor, three miles south-east of Camelford, the National Trust owns 174 acres. Intended for the permanent enjoyment of the public, this memorial to the men of the 43rd (Wessex) Division who fell in the Second World War must have caused many people to reflect on those questions of life and death affecting all organisms.

Once regarded as a treeless waste, Bodmin Moor now has some trees, mainly hardy spruce planted by the Forestry Commission on some of the limited area of enclosed land that was available for afforestation. Halvana Forest Trail near Five Lanes on the A30 passes through conifer woods established on the rough moorland grazing of a typical Bodmin Moor farm acquired by the Forestry Commission more than forty years ago. There are old mine workings, places attractive to badgers, and one has opportunities to learn of damage caused by wind in the plantations and of ways in which management of moorland can benefit farmers by improving the grazing and foresters by removing dense and inflammable gorse and other vegetation. Obviously such changes affect wildlife in several ways and do not always please naturalists.

Change of the startling type facilitated by the use of modern equipment and methods could destroy the unique heathlands of the Lizard peninsula of Cornwall. The Nature Conservancy Council is alert to this and concerned that it would now be possible to remove the 'crousair' boulders from some of them as a preliminary to drainage and cultivation. In 1974 the Council purchased 103 acres of heathland on Goonhilly Downs, Mullion. Declared a National Nature Reserve, the area has since been extended by the acquisition of a further 102 acres to help safeguard this type of habitat much of whose vegetation, including rare and uncommon plants, resembles that of the Mediterranean region. The National Trust also plays an important part here, owning land on the Lizard Downs and Lower Predannack Downs, some let to the Cornwall Naturalists' Trust.

This County Trust, though comparatively young, has made great efforts to acquire suitable properties as nature reserves, achieving splendid cooperation with the Duchy of Cornwall, Forestry Commission, National Trust and other owners. Various types of wildlife find sanctuary in Cornwall's winding lanes and steep wooded valleys, in and around its moorland streams, and even on neglected land and ruined buildings that once served its tin and china-clay industries.

The Cornwall Naturalists' Trust (CNT) has appreciated that the value of such places to wildlife is increased, their continued existence made more certain when they are given the status of protected and wardened areas. In a part of Cornwall where many similar valleys are threatened by drainage and reclamation, the County Trust owns 20 acres of Ventongimps Moor. At this SSSI near Perranporth dry heath on the higher ground gives way to wet heath and bog, and there is wet ground with alders and willows along the stream. Other CNT valley reserves are Pelyne (Lanreath) and Porthcothan Valley (St Eval), each with several types of habitat, woodland, meadow, stream and old quarry being represented in the last-named.

Much of the West Country's magnificent coastline has been secured by the National Trust and its supporters for the permanent enjoyment of the public who may also walk along the South-west Peninsula Coast Path. Starting at Minehead in Somerset, this runs along the north coast, passes round Land's End, and continues back along the south coast to the Devon–Dorset border, a total of 445 miles, finally extending along the Dorset coast for another 72 miles.

On the Somerset coast the bold headland of Brean Down, already mentioned, is an important refuge for migrating birds in spring and autumn. The STNC and its voluntary helpers have done much cutting, beating and burning here, to make fire-breaks and to control scrub and other invaders of the shallow limestone soil, the habitat of several 'chalk plants'. To the south, Bridgwater Bay, Britain's main moulting ground for shelduck in autumn, is bordered by Brean and Berrow sand-dunes, a large part of which has been declared a SSSI by the Nature Conservancy Council. In certain places marram grass and sea buckthorn have been planted to help stabilize the sand, but the pressure of visitors is making this difficult and helping to cause erosion.

Further along the coast the tidal mud-flats and salt-marshes of Bridgwater Bay National Nature Reserve are intended to be an undisturbed feeding and roosting ground for waders and wildfowl. Stert and Fenning Islands are within this 6,323-acre reserve. In the Dunster area the low coast is of particular interest to bird-watchers in winter. Minehead is just outside Exmoor National Park, but the coastline between this attractive holiday town and Combe Martin forms its northern border, one marked by steep rugged cliffs for most of its length.

Rising from the shingle beach at Minehead, North Hill, site of a nature trail and numerous woodland and moorland walks, stretches to Selworthy Beacon and Bossington Hill. Below this high ground there is a two-mile gap in the cliffs where an area of low-lying farmland is bordered by shallow pools, the haunt of duck and waders, and the stony beach of Porlock Bay. Above the valley the cliffs, now wooded, continue to Foreland Point. There is National Trust land on this bleak headland and also where the Lyn rivers rush through steep wooded valleys to unite in Lynmouth and pour through a short gap in the cliffs.

The National Trust owns moorland, cliff and woodland on the steep slopes from Wringapeak Point down to Woody Bay, and in the Heddon Valley, a Site of Special Scientific Interest, leading down to Heddon's Mouth. Footpaths following both banks of the River Heddon between Hunter's Inn and the sea enable visitors to enjoy a circular walk of about two miles. Beyond the river-gap of Heddon's Mouth, on a stretch of coast noted for its sea-bird colonies, the National Trust holds land on Holdstone Down, moorland rising to 1,145 ft, and the Great Hangman (1,046 ft), not far from Wild Pear Beach and the boundary of Exmoor National Park.

From the western outskirts of Ilfracombe to Lee there is more land owned by this body, which also manages in the public interest most of the six-mile stretch of coast between Lee Bay and Putsborough, including the headlands of Bull, Morte and Baggy Points. Between Morte Point, a SSSI, and Baggy Point the line of cliffs is interrupted by Woolacombe Sand, a sandy beach backed by sand-dunes. There has been considerable erosion of these dunes close to the main car parks, but the National Trust, in its efforts to restore

Braunton Burrows National Nature Reserve.
The plant and animal life of this vast dune system are of international scientific interest.

stability, has erected fencing, put down boardwalks and planted marram grass. Pressure from holidaymakers also occurs at Croyde Bay, between the headlands of Baggy Point and Saunton Down, and here too widespread erosion followed destruction of vegetation covering the dunes.

Behind the sandy beach extending from Saunton Down to the Taw–Torridge Estuary the sand-dunes of Braunton Burrows cover 2,275 acres and in places reach over 100 ft in height. This vast dune system, whose plant and animal life are of international scientific interest, is subject to wind erosion along its seaward edge and has suffered from heavy use around Saunton Sands car park in the north and Crow Point in the south. The southern part of the Burrows is a National Nature Reserve of 1,492 acres. Though certain areas are liable to closure for military training, the reserve is open to horse-riders along scheduled bridleways and visitors on foot who, for obvious reasons, should keep to boarded footpaths. The northern part of Braunton Burrows has been notified by the Nature Conservancy Council as a SSSI, as have parts of Saunton Sands and Saunton Raised Beach.

At Northam Burrows, on the southern side of the Taw–Torridge Estuary, Devon County Council has established a Country Park of 653 acres as a major

The Helford River whose beautiful estuary has some fine wooded scenery.

recreation area. From Westward Ho! where the National Trust owns the gorsy Kipling Tors, flat-topped cliffs stretch, almost without a break, to Hartland Point. Along this coast the National Trust safeguards cliff, farmland and woodland at its Brownsham and Beckland Cliffs properties, leasing 75 acres to the DTNC as an educational nature reserve, and at East Titchberry Farm where another mile of cliff is included.

The line of cliffs, interrupted by such natural features as rocky and sandy coves ('porths'), continues almost all the way from Hartland Point to Land's End. Long stretches of this cliffland, with its rough, broken and gorsy patches, and sometimes adjoining pasture and farmland, are owned by the National Trust and are open to the public at all times, subject to the needs of farming, forestry and the protection of wildlife. There is such access to cliff-tops from Duckpool to Sandymouth and also along the beautiful Coombe Valley, which reaches the sea at Duckpool from Kilkhampton. Here the Coombe Valley Nature Trail passes through woodland and by a stream where otters used to play. Then there are Trust properties from Northcott Mouth to Maer Cliff (adjoining Bude), at the wild headland of The Dizzard, and from Pencannow Point ('Penkenna') to Rusey Cliff, including High Cliff (731 ft), all with features to interest naturalists of all types.

South of Boscastle, where there is National Trust land on cliffs adjoining the small harbour, breeding sea-birds increase both in number and variety. Cliff ledges are, for geological reasons, larger and more numerous, and there are many off-shore stacks and islets, all providing nesting sites. The rocky coast is broken where the River Camel flows into Padstow Bay. Ornithologically the Camel estuary, with its tidal marshes, is of considerable importance. The Cornwall Bird-watching and Preservation Society has its Walmsley sanctuary, a refuge for wintering white-fronted geese, between Trewornan Bridge and Chapel Amble, and a hide near Burniere Point. Botanically the estuary has attracted attention largely because of the plants colonising its sand-dunes.

Despite development in places, the beautiful coast beyond Padstow has much to offer the naturalist. Trethias Island, a property of the Cornwall Bird-watching and Preservation Society, is a sanctuary for breeding sea-birds. North of this is Constantine Bay and south of it Porthcothan, site of sand-dunes where plants with colourful flowers grow among species that are much less attractive but nevertheless vital stabilizers of sand. One recalls that choughs, those lively red-billed, red-legged birds, once haunted the cliffs hereabouts, their last Cornish base.

South of the cliffs and sandy beaches extending from Bedruthan to Newquay is the Gannel estuary where the National Trust Cubert and Gannel properties include saltings and sand-dunes. Between this area and Perranporth are extensive dunes whose sands long ago buried St Pirans Oratory, now an ancient monument.

Access to St Agnes Beacon (629 ft) enables naturalists not only to explore 61 acres of heathy ground but also to enjoy some magnificent views. There is access to another 363 acres of cliff and moorland just along the coast at Chapel Coombe, scene of tin and copper mining until the 1920s, where one may walk down to the small cove of Chapel Porth.

Almost the entire coast from Portreath to Godrevy on the east coast of St

Ives Bay is owned by the National Trust whose tenants farm the flat-topped cliffs for much of the six-mile stretch. Many bird-watchers are particularly fond of the part from Hell's Mouth to Godrevy Point. The River Hayle enters St Ives Bay, whose surrounding sandy beaches and extensive dunes (The Towans) are heavily used during the holiday season, through an estuary where some salt-marsh has developed. A good place in autumn for waders, the Hayle estuary has suffered much from human activity in recent years, a situation over which the Cornwall Bird-watching and Preservation Society has expressed great concern. St Ives Island or Head, on the extreme west of the Bay, is an excellent point for sea-bird watching, especially after autumn gales. (It is an interesting experience to listen to serious sea watchers bemoaning the lack of 'good gales'!)

Along the granite cliffs from St Ives westwards to Land's End much of the land below the bold, irregular granite uplands is occupied by small farms. The coast path enables one to walk round this part of Land's End Peninsula (and, of course, round the remainder, too) and there is access to National Trust land at Zennor Head, Rosemergy and Trevean Cliffs, and between Sennen Cove and Land's End at Mayon and Trevescan Cliffs.

Four miles south-east of Land's End, on a stretch of coast where streams flow quickly through narrow valleys to the sea, headland, cove and valley from Treen Cliff to Penberth Cove are in National Trust ownership. East of Penzance, Marazion Marsh, a fresh marsh with reedbed, is visited by waders on passage, wintering divers and grebe, and occasionally 'rarities'. Conservation work has been carried out here by the Cornwall Bird-watching and Preservation Society to safeguard this important site and ensure that it does not dry out.

Moving along the coast, one reaches Porthleven and a mile further on Loe Pool (The Loe). Surrounded by woods and farmland, this long freshwater lake, a haunt of wintering duck, is separated from the sea by Loe Bar, a mass of shingle thrown up by the waves. Between this National Trust estate of 1,536 acres and Lizard Point, the most southerly part of England, the flat-topped cliffs are broken by small coves where streams run into the sea. Warm-toned serpentine cliffs occur here and also on the other side of the Point where an irregular coastline, with coves and rocks, eventually leads to the beautiful estuary of the Helford River whose fine wooded scenery is always delightful, some compensation for tree-loving bird-watchers when birds are scarce.

Just along the coast, below Falmouth and St Mawes, is the mouth of the estuary where the combined waters of the River Fal and the Truro and Tresillian Rivers meet the sea. These rivers and their muddy side-creeks form what is virtually a complex of small estuaries. Here, in undisturbed backwaters sheltered by well-wooded banks, waders and wildfowl rest and feed. Some of these birds are attracted to foreshore and mud-flats in the nature reserve established below Ruan Lanihorne as the result of cooperation between the National Trust and the Cornwall Naturalists' Trust.

Between Nare Head and Dodman Point, a good place for sea-watching ornithologists, lies Veryan Bay, site of the Gull Rock, the only really important breeding site for sea-birds along this somewhat gentle southern coast (gentler than Cornwall's northern coast!). This particular section of West Country coast may not excite many naturalists but those with time and patience will eventually reap their reward, for creatures and plants of interest to true naturalists, those who do not concentrate on 'rarities', are to be found here. For this reason, the Fowey and Looe estuaries, though often regarded as of minor importance, are worth visiting at quiet times by those who are not in a hurry.

Plymouth Sound is the entrance to a great wetlands complex, the estuaries of the Rivers Tamar, Tavy, Lynher and Plym. Mud-flat, salt-marsh and reedbed are among the habitats and several SSSIs have been notified to the local authorities by the Nature Conservancy Council. Apart from its value as a place where long-term studies are made by botanists and marine biologists, the whole area is of much ornithological interest. Wintering birds include wildfowl, and avocets, black-tailed godwits and other waders. Other birds are seen here on spring and autumn passage, and there are, of course, a number of resident species.

A reserve extending from Cargreen to Skinham Point and including Kingsmill Lake is run by the CNT, while a small woodland reserve on steep cliffs overlooking the Tamar and above Weir Quay is managed by the DTNC, which cooperates with the Plymouth City Museum in the management of an Educational Nature Reserve, comprising woodland, stream, pond and tidal mud-flats, at Warleigh Point. The small Plym Estuary is virtually a public nature reserve, for its wintering waders and wildfowl and other birds may be observed from a lay-by on the A38.

A few miles further along the South Devon coast, and only five miles from the centre of Plymouth, is the Yealm estuary whose fourteen-mile shoreline is wooded for about half of its length. Biologists have long valued this estuary for its varied marine flora and fauna, and ornithologists have recorded 144 species of birds in the area during the past five years. Many other organisms occur, but sadly there are signs that marine life may be suffering from the effect of pollution and birds (and possibly other forms of animal life) from the noise of outboard motors. Realizing that the situation could quickly deteriorate even further, Devon County Council has, with praiseworthy concern for wildlife, expressed the hope that everything possible will be done to maintain the rural character of the estuary area.

The estuaries of the Rivers Erme and Avon, whose mouths open on to Bigbury Bay, are often considered to be of minor interest. But, here again, so much depends on the time available and the extent to which naturalists wish to explore particular areas. In the past the Avon may have run into the sea through what is now called Kingsbridge Estuary, a drowned river valley into which no large river now flows. Be this as it may, there is no doubt that this wetland area, with its narrow, rocky entrance and muddy creeks, is well worth the attention of naturalists, especially those who enjoy watching wintering waders and wildfowl. Starting from Charleton village, near Kingsbridge, one may walk a footpath trail that eventually runs along the side of Frogmore Creek and passes Wareham Point (good for bird-watching) before returning to Charleton Marsh and the village. There is also access to about eleven miles of cliffland owned by the National Trust, about six miles being between Bolt Tail and Bolt Head, on the western side of Salcombe harbour, entrance to Kingsbridge Estuary, and over five miles from Mill Bay to Venerick's Cove on the other side.

Past Prawle Point and Start Point, favourite places for bird-watching, is

Slapton. Here, in a comparatively small area, are Slapton Ley Nature Reserve, the Field Studies Council's Slapton Ley Field Study Centre and the Slapton Bird Observatory of the Devon Bird-watching and Preservation Society. Divided into Higher Ley, silted-up and reed-grown, and Lower Ley, a large body of natural freshwater, Slapton Ley is separated from the sea by the sand and shingle bar of Slapton Sands. In addition to habitats already mentioned, the Slapton Ley area, a SSSI, includes woods, banks, hedgerows and scrub, all providing food and shelter and helping to encourage a greater variety of wildlife.

The beautiful wooded estuary of the River Dart, near whose mouth the DTNC has two reserves of woodland, scrub and cliff, was used as winter quarters by spoonbills. Nowadays bird-watchers have to be content with commoner species for much of the time. Sea-birds nest at Scabbacombe Head and also at Berry Head, the limestone headland, now a Local Nature Reserve, whose plants have long interested botanists.

Much of the coast from Berry Head to Dawlish Warren has been developed, but there are places that retain a real interest for naturalists. For example, Hope's Nose and Anstey's Cove have colonies of kittiwakes. The Teign Estuary, its wide mud-flats the regular feeding grounds of several common waders, waterfowl and other birds, is visited in autumn and winter by such other species as goldeneye, red-breasted merganser, grey plover, black-tailed and bar-tailed godwits, ruff and avocet.

Even more important to birds are the great estuary of the River Exe and its adjoining marshes. Species resident in the area are joined by summer visitors and birds on passage, and in winter by large flocks of dunlin, oystercatchers, dark-bellied Brent geese and wigeon and smaller numbers of such attractive birds as avocets.

Dawlish Warren, the double sand spit across the mouth of the Exe, is not only a favourite observation point for bird-watchers, but the only British site for the sand (or warren) crocus (*Romulea*). The future of this very small plant, which also occurs in the Channel Islands, along the western coasts of Europe and nearly all around the Mediterranean, is now in the hands of the DTNC. The Trust now owns the Warren Crocus Company whose main asset is Dawlish Inner Warren, an area of grassy, stabilized dunes, where the Warren Golf Club has pursued its activities for many years without harming the sand crocus or other scarce plants growing there.

Its smallness should not lead naturalists into thinking that the Otter Estuary, east of Budleigh Salterton, is an area that can safely be ignored. It is, in fact, an excellent place for studying the vegetation and development of salt-marsh and for observing the many birds attracted to its mud-flats and neighbouring meadows. East of Sidmouth, at Salcombe Hill Cliff, Dunscombe Cliff and Weston Mouth, the DTNC watches over nature reserves consisting mainly of cliff face where 'slipped' areas have been colonized by shrubs and trees. A two-and-a-half-mile nature trail starts from the car park at the top of Salcombe Hill, passing among trees and along the cliff path. Springs issuing from the greensand where it joins less pervious marl help to diversify the flora and not only flowering plants but ferns, fungi, mosses, liverworts and lichens grow here.

Almost the most westerly 'chalkland' in Britain, the chalk cliffs and undercliff along this coast have an interesting flora. Beer Head itself, also with chalk

Left Burgh Island on the Devon coast. Here, as on so many cliffs, ledges are used by sea-birds and plants (thrift is seen on the right of the picture).

plants, is a good observation point for bird-watchers and the Axe Estuary, though small, attracts waders, wildfowl and other birds.

The five-mile length of coast between the mouth of the River Axe and the outskirts of Lyme Regis forms Axmouth–Lyme Regis Undercliffs National Nature Reserve. Although the reserve is of considerable interest for its geological strata and fossil-bearing rocks, land-slipping and the subsequent colonization of the broken ground by plants are what make this wild area especially fascinating. Ashwood developed naturally in the wide ravine that appeared between Dowlands and Bindon after the great landslip of 1839, many other plants have gained footholds where lesser landslips have occurred more recently, and plants will undoubtedly cover future scars inevitably resulting from the geological structure of the cliffs.

ISLANDS

Off the coast of the West Country are a number of islands supporting animal and plant life of many types. Pride of place must surely be given to the Isles of Scilly, granite islands forming an archipelago some twenty-eight miles south-west of Land's End. Here five inhabited islands, about forty uninhabited islands carrying vegetation and a large number of bare rocks are arranged in an oval group measuring roughly eleven miles by five. Mild winters, cool summers, high humidity, strong winds, a good sunshine record and other factors combine to produce conditions that are in many ways unique in Britain. Exotic plant species thrive, those in the sub-tropical gardens on Tresco being especially noteworthy, and its position makes Scilly important as a resting- and feeding-place for birds on passage and as a landfall for vagrants (American species and other rarities).

The types of habitat present in Scilly include cliff, shore and dunes, maritime heath and granite outcrops, ponds, pools and freshwater marshes, copses and shelterbelts, and cultivated areas. There are two nature trails on St Mary's, the largest inhabited island, which is about two and a quarter miles long. Other recognized trails may be followed on this and the other inhabited islands The uninhabited islands, all natural sanctuaries for wildlife, may be visited but certain restrictions are enforced between 15 April and 20 July (naturalists wishing to visit during this period should consult the Duchy of Cornwall's Warden, Hugh House, St Mary's, well in advance. See also the Duchy's booklet *The Isles of Scilly: nature trails and wildlife conservation*).

The island of Lundy, a granite mass, lies eleven miles north of Hartland Point and twenty-two miles from Ilfracombe, the nearest port. Despite its smallness (three miles long, four-fifths of a mile at its widest), it is a place of great fascination for naturalists. Its coastline of a little over eight miles includes precipitous cliffs, deep gullies and grassy slopes and, in places, provides nesting-sites for numerous sea-birds. Rising above cliffs and steep sidelands the island plateau reaches 459 ft at its highest point. Among the varied habitats of Lundy's 1,062 acres are pasture and rough grazing, disused quarries, moorland, bog, peaty banks and rhododendron thickets. Broad-leaved trees and conifers are also present, mainly in the south of the island, some standing up well to the strong salt winds. Like many of the other plants, they must at various times have been seriously affected by introduced goats and rabbits.

In 1947, with the generous cooperation of the then owner, Martin Coles Harman, a London businessman who had loved Lundy for many years, the Lundy Field Society was established to encourage the study of the island's natural history. This it continues to do with the support of the present owner, the National Trust, and its lessee, the Landmark Trust.

Over the years much attention has been paid to the island's birds. Many have been trapped or netted at migration times, ringed and then released, and details of individuals subsequently recovered or 'controlled' (examined and then released) have been published in the Lundy Field Society's annual reports. Certain other forms of animal life have been studied, as have the plants, including the unique Lundy cabbage. In recent years much time and effort have been devoted to the marine plants and animals living around Lundy, and an area of the surrounding sea will be managed as far as practicable as a nature reserve.

A limestone mass three-quarters of a mile in length, Steep Holm, already mentioned, lies in the middle of the Bristol Channel about five miles off Weston-super-Mare. Declared a SSSI by the Nature Conservancy Council, it was bought by the Kenneth Allsop Memorial Trust in 1976, as a living memorial to Kenneth Allsop (1920–73), writer, broadcaster and conservationist.

Steep Holm is noted for its large colony of herring gulls (some 6,500 pairs), great and lesser black-backed gulls also being present, though in much smaller numbers. Cormorants breeding on the island's north cliffs attract much attention, as do birds on passage, many of which are ringed.

The island has a sycamore wood, an increasing mass of scrub and a large area of alexanders, a greenish-yellow-flowered plant whose stems used to be eaten like celery. Then there are such other interesting plants as the rare wild leek, caper spurge (once cultivated for its fruits) and, above all, the beautiful wild peony, a native of southern Europe.

Realizing that Steep Holm is the only place in Britain where the peony is naturalized, and that the wild cliffside population had been reduced to a single plant, the Kenneth Allsop Memorial Trust has harvested seed and planted part of it on rocky cliff ledges on the island. Another batch was sown in a mainland garden from which seedlings will eventually be transferred to Steep Holm. Here, as elsewhere, visitors should do everything possible to help conserve not only rarities but the entire fauna and flora. The word visitors includes scientists, naturalists, photographers and—dare one say it—experts. One makes this clear because in the 1830s Steep Holm's wild peony was nearly eradicated by 'scientists' and in recent years the antics of 'naturalists', especially those determined to photograph the peony flowers, have given cause for grave concern.

Mammals

Many British mammals are mainly active by night and so, not surprisingly, there may be visitors and residents, too, who find some difficulty in believing that more than forty species live in the West Country.

As in so many other places, evidence of the presence of the hedgehog *Erinaceus europaeus* is often seen in the form of remains of individuals killed on the roads. Modern traffic takes a heavy toll of this species, the only spiny British mammal. Hedgehogs will eat carrion and they take a comparatively small number of game-birds' eggs, but beetles, caterpillars, slugs, earthworms and other invertebrates seem to interest them far more. In their turn, hedgehogs may be killed by man and by tawny owls, foxes, badgers and dogs. Often regarded as a species of deciduous woodland, the hedgehog may also be found in scrub, hedgerows, large and somewhat neglected gardens and other places with sufficient low cover for shelter and nesting. Sheltered nests are particularly

Pygmy shrew. This small mammal usually lives among low vegetation, but it has also been found in nest boxes well above the ground.

important for hibernation from about October to early April, a time when many hedgehogs die.

Another insectivore living in the West Country is the mole *Talpa europaea*, a velvety furred animal well adapted for subterranean life. This species is rarely seen on the surface, but mole-hills, mounds of soil pushed up during tunnelling, reveal its presence, most noticeably in pastures, less so in deciduous woodland, where ridges of soil indicate tunnelling close to the surface and where fortresses, large mounds containing nesting chambers, are sometimes found. Moles eat earthworms, insect larvae and other small creatures found in soil. Their tunnelling sometimes helps to drain land, but farmers often regard them as pests, their mounds being a nuisance in places where machinery is used to cut grass for hay or silage. Moles are also caught and killed by foxes, cats and birds of prey. Their more interesting West Country habitats include cliff-tops and

The noctule, a large bat that roosts in tree holes.

stretches of stony soil near the shore at the Axmouth–Lyme Regis Undercliffs National Nature Reserve.

This reserve is among the haunts of common, pygmy and water shrews, as are Dartmoor and Exmoor National Parks. The common shrew *Sorex araneus* and the pygmy shrew *S. minutus* occur in cover provided by thick grass, scrub and other low vegetation, feeding on earthworms, beetles and such other invertebrates as spiders and woodlice. Their main predators are owls, though cats will also kill them. These shrews, with their quiet twittering and shrill screams, are more often heard than seen. In time patient observers are, however, rewarded, as was the case when H. G. Hurrell, the distinguished West Country naturalist, found pygmy shrews occupying nest-boxes ten feet above the ground.

The water shrew *Neomys fodiens* is a good swimmer but, despite its name, it also inhabits woodland, and other places with suitable cover, well away from water. Feeding on insects, snails, small fish and frogs, water shrews are themselves eaten by owls, fish and certain mammals. Water shrew remains have been extracted from barn owl pellets (indigestible material ejected by the bird) in several parts of the West Country, and at Camelford, Cornwall, this small mammal formed one-twentieth of the barn owl's diet by prey weight.

Absent from the British mainland, the lesser white-toothed shrew *Crocidura suaveolens* lives among seashore rocks and in vegetation on many of the Isles of Scilly. Insects and amphipods are eaten by the Scilly shrew, as the species is often called, and its own numbers are believed to be kept in check by such predators as birds of prey and domestic cats.

Turning to the Chiroptera (=hand-wing), we find that about twelve species of bats, the only mammals capable of true flight, have been recorded from the West Country. Protected by the Conservation of Wild Creatures and Wild Plants Act 1975, the greater horseshoe bat *Rhinolophus ferrumequinum* has been recorded from all three counties of the region. It roosts in the roofs of old houses and barns in summer and hibernates in caves, rock fissures and mine tunnels during the winter. Disturbance by people entering caves during the critical period of hibernation has led conservation bodies to safeguard several sites and to close entrances by steel grilles. This has been done with the aid of a grant from the World Wildlife Fund at Higher Kiln Quarry, Buckfastleigh, a disused limestone quarry owned by the Society for the Promotion of Nature Conservation and managed by the Devon Trust for Nature Conservation as a closed reserve. The lesser horseshoe bat *R. hipposideros* has also been recorded from the West Country, where it and the greater horseshoe bat have been known to hibernate in caves and rock fissures in Ebbor Gorge National Nature Reserve.

The whiskered bat *Myotis mystacinus* has been confused with its close relative Brandt's bat *M. brandti*, but, though their distribution patterns are even less perfectly known than those of many other bats, both species live in Devon and there is a positive record of Brandt's bat from Somerset. Natterer's bat *M. nattereri*, with its broad, pointed wings, is known from the region, including Devon, in which county the skeleton of an individual of this species was extracted from a barn owl pellet. There are authentic records of Bechstein's bat *M. bechsteini*, a forest bat whose summer and winter roosts are often in tree

This brown hare is crouching in its form, a shallow depression in the grass.

holes, from Somerset and Devon, and Daubenton's bat *M. daubentoni*, a species of wooded country, also occurs in the region.

The noctule *Nyctalus noctula*, a large bat that is fond of roosting in tree holes, is another member of the West Country fauna. The skeleton of one individual was found in a barn owl pellet at Tavistock, Devon. A small species of various types of habitat, the pipistrelle *Pipistrellus pipistrellus* is often considered to be the commonest West Country bat. Much less is known about the distribution of the barbastelle *Barbastella barbastellus*, whose broad black ears are joined across the forehead, a feature exclusive to this bat. The common long-eared bat *Plecotus auritus* lives in Dartmoor National Park, Axmouth–Lyme Regis Undercliffs National Nature Reserve, and other parts of the region. Its close relative the grey long-eared bat *P. austriacus* has not so far been recorded from the West Country.

Bats are harmless creatures that feed on insects and spiders, and everything possible should be done to ensure their protection.

The Lagomorphs, small plant-eaters, are represented in the region by the rabbit and the brown hare. Despite the attacks of man and other predators and the ravages of myxomatosis, the disease that seriously affected the species in the 1950s and now occurs annually in many places, the rabbit *Oryctolagus cuniculus* still occurs in some numbers. It is present not only on the mainland but on Steep Holm, where many individuals have reddish markings behind the ears, a characteristic noticed some 150 years ago, and on the Isles of Scilly and Lundy.

Rabbits have a well-deserved reputation as pests of agriculture, horticulture and forestry. In the wild they affect the lives and activities of many other living things, playing an important part, for example, in maintaining certain habitats. The extent of their contribution to the well-being of the large blue butterfly, a species that has sadly declined and is now protected by the Conservation of Wild Creatures and Wild Plants Act 1975, has gradually become apparent. It is now appreciated that rabbits (and other grazing animals) prevent coarse plants from ousting thyme, whose flowers and seed are eaten by the butterfly's young larvae. By keeping vegetation short, rabbits also create conditions suitable for the sun-loving *Myrmica* ants which carry the larvae of the large blue butterfly to their underground nests. Here the butterfly larvae feed on ant grubs, hibernate and later pupate, the winged butterflies emerging in June.

The brown hare *Lepus capensis* feeds on farm crops, bark from young trees, grass and other wild plants. With a somewhat patchy distribution pattern in the West Country, Lively Puss, as the hare has been called, may be seen on Exmoor, Dartmoor, farmland and sand-dunes, and in Axmouth–Lyme Regis Undercliffs National Nature Reserve and certain other nature reserves.

Most of the fifteen British species of rodents have been recorded from the region, but there is much doubt as to the numbers of some of them. Anxiety would undoubtedly be the proper word to use when speaking of the status in the West Country of the red squirrel *Sciurus vulgaris*. According to the distribution map in *The Handbook of British Mammals* (1977), its last stronghold here was the extreme west of Cornwall. Some people think that the species may be holding out in some remote place, but sadly it seems likely that the red squirrel has vanished from this part of England.

The grey squirrel *S. carolinensis*, which has replaced the red squirrel over so much of the country, is active in all three counties of the region, and its large dreys, or nests, of dead leaves, grass and sticks are a common sight in many stretches of woodland. The main invasion of the West Country by this introduced species seems to have started during the 1950s, but even in the late 1960s it was still not widespread in Cornwall. A pest of forestry, the grey squirrel damages trees by stripping bark from the stems. Beech and sycamore are particularly susceptible to attack, especially at the pole-stage, and these trees have suffered damage at, for example, the Long Wood reserve, where the Somerset Trust for Nature Conservation has resorted to trapping grey squirrels.

National campaigns to exterminate the species have failed, due, among other factors, to its ability to produce two litters, each averaging three young, per season, the apparent ease with which it can adapt itself to life in both rural and urban situations and its mobility. Certain of the grey squirrel's feeding habits affect farmers, gardeners and game interests, but there is no doubt that acorns, beech and hazel nuts and other types of tree mast, buds, shoots and leaves of trees and smaller plants and certain toadstools are basic items of diet in this country. Man is probably the species' most important predator in the region, but individuals, mainly young ones, are killed by stoats, foxes, birds of prey and even cats and dogs.

A common and widespread West Country mammal, the bank vole *Clethrionomys glareolus* is also given the name of red-backed vole, a most appropriate alternative. Living in tunnels and in runways through thick cover in woodland,

Grey squirrel, the introduced species that has replaced the indigenous red squirrel over much of Britain.

The water vole's diet consists chiefly of grasses, but this one was feeding on a dead perch.

scrub, grassland and hedges, this little animal does not attract much attention. The bank vole's food consists largely of fruits, seeds and leaves and in hard winters it may bark young trees and shrubs to get at the moist cambium layer. Weasels are among its most important predators, as are birds of prey.

The field vole *Microtus agrestis*, another common and widespread West Country mammal, is, as its name suggests, a species of open places, especially rough, tussocky grassland and young, grassy plantations. An active little animal, sometimes referred to as the short-tailed vole or field mouse, it feeds mainly on the leaves and stems of grasses, causing significant damage on occasion. The diets of many species of birds and mammals include field voles, whose fluctuations in numbers, the so-called plagues and crashes, undoubtedly have serious effects on the habits and numbers of predators. Mammalian predators comprise foxes, stoats and weasels, while birds taking field voles include kestrels, buzzards, owls and herons.

Often called the water rat, an unfortunate choice of name because it is certainly not a rat, the water vole *Arvicola terrestris* lives quietly among waterside vegetation and in tunnels in banks of rivers, ditches and ponds. Quiet and patient observers will eventually see it swimming and diving or come across it feeding in characteristic hunch-backed attitude, a stem of grass or rush held in its fore-paws. Like so many other species, the water vole has its predators, pike, stoat and mink among them, and suffers from destruction and severe modification of its haunts.

Wood mouse, also called long-tailed field mouse. This small mammal has many enemies.

The wood mouse (also called long-tailed field mouse) *Apodemus sylvaticus* occurs in many parts of the West Country, including Tresco and St Marys in the Isles of Scilly, being found among rocks, even those near the tops of Dartmoor tors, and in woodland, hedges, fields and gardens where there is suitable cover and litter under which to make runways and nests. Tree seeds, seedlings, fungi, fruits, centipedes and insect larvae are among many items forming its varied diet. The wood mouse itself is eaten by owls and kestrels and such mammals as foxes, badgers, cats and stoats.

Distinguished from other mice by its yellow collar (and certain other characteristics), the yellow-necked mouse *A. flavicollis* is believed to occur in rare or scattered colonies in the region, though further detailed studies of this species are obviously needed.

A somewhat elusive species, our smallest British rodent, the harvest mouse *Micromys minutus*, is an attractive member of the West Country fauna whose status has caused concern in recent years. The red mouse, as this species is also known, is not, it appears, such a rare animal as many people had supposed. Among records of its presence are those from Sedgemoor (wet pastures and hedgerows), Axmouth–Lyme Regis Undercliffs National Nature Reserve and grassland on the Mendips. Other evidence has taken the form of ginger-red fur and hard parts of harvest mice taken from barn owl pellets collected in the three counties of the region. Nowadays, with cereal fields much less suitable for the species, harvest mice are more likely to be found in rough grassy places,

Here seen in wheat, the harvest mouse, our smallest British rodent, makes good use of its prehensile tail.

Given the right conditions, the common or brown rat, a recognized pest, may breed continuously. This one is seen with a large litter.

reedbeds, ditches and hedgerows, where their breeding nests are built well above ground level among the stalks of tall, dense vegetation. Besides seeds and berries, harvest mice eat insects. They themselves are taken by certain larger mammals and by barn owls, mentioned earlier, other owls and hawks.

Some of these creatures also prey on the house mouse *Mus musculus*, a species long associated with human settlements and one that is far more numerous than many people realize. Besides eating much intended for consumption by humans and livestock, house mice, whose disease-carrying potential should not be overlooked, contaminate large quantities of food.

Nowadays little is heard or seen of the ship rat *Rattus rattus*, the so-called black rat, many examples of which are, in fact, brown. Four were captured on Lundy in April 1971, when two members of the department of biological sciences of the University of Exeter made a preliminary survey of the island's rats. The ship rats' stomachs contained vegetable matter together with mollusc and insect remains. The stomachs of ten common rats *R. norvegicus* caught by these investigators on Lundy contained far less vegetable material but remains of insects, crustacea, centipedes and a young mammal, probably a rabbit, were present. No signs of bird remains were found in any of the stomachs and it was thought most unlikely that the rat populations at the 1971 levels would affect the numbers of burrow-nesting birds, puffins and manx shearwaters, on Lundy.

The common rat (also called the brown rat) is a widespread member of the West Country fauna, one whose numbers on farms and in urban areas may well depend on such factors as the time of year and the nature of any control measures in force. A recognized pest, it destroys and soils vital food supplies and carries leptospirosis, which is transmissible to man, and some other diseases. Rats, particularly young ones, are eaten by foxes, badgers, weasels, owls and other predators.

Certain of these species also prey on the dormouse *Muscardinus avellanarius*, a harmless small mammal of coppice, old and well-established hedgerows and deciduous woodland, places where shrubs and scrub provide cover and where such food items as nuts, berries and the leaves and flowers of honeysuckle are available. A nocturnal creature and one that hibernates, though not always continuously, from about October to April, the dormouse often manages to conceal its presence in an area from all but expert naturalists. Those who took part in the Mammal Society's dormouse survey have shown that the species still occurs in many parts of the West Country. It is an agile climber and, not surprisingly, it has sometimes been found in bird nest-boxes well above the ground.

The fox *Vulpes vulpes*, Britain's only wild representative of the Canidae, the dog family, is abundant and widespread on the West Country mainland.

Dormouse, a harmless small mammal that still occurs in many parts of the West Country.

Nowadays this species is not only at home in rural areas but also in urban situations (in Plymouth, for example), where it employs its skill as a scavenger at dustbins and on refuse tips. Though mainly nocturnal, the fox is sometimes seen during daylight and may be disturbed while resting in bracken, gorse or some other form of ground cover. Dartmoor and Exmoor have their foxes and there are comparatively few areas of woodland, moorland, sand-dune and cliff where this active species is completely unknown. The fact that it will, on occasion, take lambs and poultry has earned the fox a bad name, and there is concern among gamekeepers and conservationists when it attacks ground-nesting birds. Yet, important as they are to the people concerned, these creatures form only a small part of the diets of some foxes.

In addition to carrion, scavenged foods and the items just mentioned, foxes will eat earthworms, field voles and other small rodents, rabbits and hares, small birds, insects, fruits and berries. The extent to which they prey on hares does not seem to be known, but one recalls that, early in the nineteenth century, George Templar, a West Country friend of the famous sporting parson Jack Russell (whose name is borne by a breed of terriers), is said to have hunted hares with a pack of foxes. While they will occasionally dig their own earths or enlarge rabbit burrows for this purpose, foxes are content to make use of

The fox, Britain's only wild representative of the dog family. Nowadays it is at home in both rural and urban situations.

Badger emerging from its set. In Britain earthworms are the most important single food item of this species.

badger sets, sometimes sharing larger ones with the rightful occupants, the badgers.

The badger *Meles meles* occurs throughout the mainland of the West Country, being much more common in some parts than in others. As a rule, sets are excavated in well drained and easily worked soils, often in deciduous woods and copses, hedgerows and scrub. Such other places as Mendip caves and Cornish mine workings are also used, and a few sets are sited on open moorland on, for example, Dartmoor. During the summer months badgers usually remain in their sets until sunset and at other times of year they stay there until darkness has fallen. On occasion, however, visitors to the more secluded parts of the West Country may see them during the hours of daylight. This was the case when, one sunny August morning, people travelling on a launch off the Cornish coast were able to watch a badger walking along the cliff.

Badgers eat many different kinds of both animal and plant foods, those taken at any one time depending largely on availability but also on weather conditions and other factors. In Britain earthworms are the most important single food item and, in Somerset, Dr Ernest Neal, a leading authority on badgers, examined several stomachs containing over 200 of them. Larvae, pupae and adult beetles, wasps and many other insects, young rabbits, rats and other mammals, fruits and such cereals as oats and wheat are also among the species' main foods. Carrion, green plants, birds, molluscs, reptiles and amphibians are also taken and may, in certain circumstances, be consumed in significant amounts.

It would be idle to pretend that the feeding habits of badgers never give farmers, smallholders and poultry-keepers cause for concern. The killing of lambs and poultry is certainly not typical of the species, but individuals engaging in this kind of destruction, often old or sick animals, certainly get badgers a very bad name in certain quarters. The whole question of the different attitudes of people over badger damage is highlighted by Derek Tangye in his enchanting book *Sun on the Lintel.* He is prepared to accept the presence of badgers on his land in Cornwall, despite the fact that they have dug in his daffodil meadows and have eaten carrots grown for his donkeys. But he obviously appreciates that a farmer who has lost a crop (and with it income) might react very differently.

Serious attention was focused on badgers in November 1976, when the Ministry of Agriculture, Fisheries and Food summarized the evidence linking bovine tuberculosis in badgers with outbreaks of the disease among cattle, a problem virtually confined to limited areas of the South-West. Two of the statutory control areas, in which sets associated with established infection in badgers are sealed and gassed by Ministry personnel, are in Cornwall and another

Weasel, a small and slender mammal that destroys large numbers of mice and voles.

is in Devon (a fourth control area, comprising parts of Avon, Gloucestershire and Wiltshire, is outside the scope of this book). In its second report (December 1977), the Ministry stated that there were signs that the measures taken were having their desired effect, the general incidence among cattle in the South West of bovine tuberculosis, a hazard not only to cattle but humans, having been somewhat reduced. After a suitable interval following eradication of the disease, healthy badgers will be allowed to reoccupy areas where the species has been eliminated. Thus the Ministry's operations may well benefit the badger's long-term future. One must add that nobody should contemplate taking action against badgers without first seeking expert advice on the laws concerning them.

The stoat *Mustela erminea* lives in many parts of the West Country, its haunts including Dartmoor and Exmoor. Expert at bounding, climbing and swimming, this active little carnivore takes birds and small mammals, including rabbits, as its main food. It has other predators but man is probably its main enemy. A smaller animal and one lacking the stoat's black tail-tip, the weasel *M. nivalis* is a widespread member of the West Country fauna. It feeds on mice and voles and will occasionally take birds and eggs.

A North American species that escaped from fur farms, the mink *M. vison* was found breeding on the upper reaches of the river Teign in Devon in 1956. Now present in many parts of Britain, it has established breeding colonies along river banks in the West Country. Despite trapping and other attempts to control its numbers, the mink appears to be flourishing in the region, where it shows little or no fear of man and is often seen. The main items of its diet in this part of Britain are moorhen, coot and other birds and small mammals. Damage by mink does not appear to have reached serious economic proportions, though one cannot overlook the concern of people whose fish, game birds and domestic livestock are attacked.

The otter *Lutra lutra*, a much larger animal than the mink, is shy and retiring and difficult to find. Although it is still present in certain West Country rivers, the species has declined not only in the region but in many other parts of the country. As a result, the otter was given total protection, under the Conservation of Wild Creatures and Wild Plants Act 1975, in England and Wales with effect from 1 January 1978. Some naturalists are anxious that this action should not divert attention from the problems of habitat destruction and disturbance, both serious threats to otters (and indeed to certain other species). What may be regarded as harmless tidying and cleaning operations may involve the removal of reedbeds, scrub and other dense waterside vegetation where otters like to make their open nests or couches. The modification of river banks, under which they have their dens or holts, also occurs. It is particularly important that such places should be left and allowed to remain undisturbed as sites for breeding, which in Britain may occur at any time of year. Another vital requirement is, of course, an adequate supply of food, whose most important element, various species of fish, is likely to be most abundant in unpolluted waters.

The common seal *Phoca vitulina* is anything but common in West Country waters and usually only single wanderers are seen there. The grey or Atlantic seal *Halichoerus grypus* breeds along parts of the Cornish coasts, on the uninhabited Western Rocks in the Isles of Scilly and on Lundy, the pups being

The head of an otter, a reminder that this species is now protected by law.

born in sea caves, on low rocky islands or on small isolated beaches backed by steep cliffs. Born in September or October or, as has been reported from Cornwall, between March and May, grey seal pups are often severely injured against rocks during gales or crushed by heavy boulders moved in big seas, many of them dying very young.

Much remains to be discovered about the movements of seals, but young grey seals marked in Pembrokeshire have been recovered at several points along West Country coasts. At one time grey seals were much persecuted, especially by Cornish inshore fishermen who killed both young and old. Now the Conservation of Seals Act 1970 protects the species from 1 September to 31 December and during this close season grey seals can be killed only under licence. Grey seals feed largely on fish and there is no doubt that they can be serious pests to fisheries, though this does not appear to be the case in West Country waters.

Porpoises, dolphins and even whales are sighted off West Country coasts or found stranded, but these entirely aquatic mammals are outside the scope of this book.

Well within it are deer, five species of which are at large in the West Country. Pride of place must surely go to the red deer *Cervus elaphus*, the largest British land mammal. Red deer live in the wooded combes and on the open moors of Exmoor National Park, on the wooded slopes of the Quantocks and in Lydford Woods in West Devon, and the species, one capable of wandering great distances, is also seen in certain of the steep wooded valleys of Cornwall. Eating many different types of vegetation, red deer enjoy fresh young grass, leaves and shoots of trees, heather and a variety of farm crops, and in winter they will dig down into snow for lichens and ferns and take ivy and holly.

After exploring likely areas, people are often surprised that they have not seen red deer. This is not surprising because these animals feed mainly at night, emerging from cover at dusk which, like dawn, is a good time to look out for them. Local residents are often prepared to help visitors who wish to watch deer and their advice will usually prove invaluable. A good pair of binoculars is essential, and one must be perfectly quiet and not wear light-coloured clothes.

The red deer is our largest British land mammal. This stag has its antlers in velvet.

Observance of these rules will also help naturalists seeking fallow deer *Dama dama*, a fairly widespread West Country species. Fallow deer may often be seen in wooded areas near old deer parks and this is certainly the case at Dunster, Combe Sydenham and Nettlecombe in Somerset. In Devon the species inhabits such places as Plym Forest, whose scattered blocks cover some two thousand acres between Tavistock and Kingston, and Dunsford Wood, a reserve of the Devon Trust for Nature Conservation that lies nine miles west of Exeter. It has also been recorded from several places in Cornwall.

Commonly with a white-spotted, rich fawn summer coat, which becomes duller, greyish and indistinctly spotted in winter, the fallow deer produces many colour varieties. Some of them occur in the West Country, sooty-black individuals and white ones being seen in, for example, north-west Somerset.

The black fallow deer has been mistaken for the sika deer *Cervus nippon*, a native of East Asia. Sika deer were kept at Pixton Park, Dulverton, until 1915, when they broke out of their paddock and established themselves in the wild. In recent years it has been suggested that this population has seriously declined and may even have become extinct. Be this as it may, the species is reported from time to time, especially from places along and around the Somerset–Devon boundary. Sika still live on Lundy, where a few were introduced in 1927. The dense rhododendron thickets provide cover from which they emerge to feed, mainly on grasses, at dusk.

Already established in many parts of Somerset and Devon, the roe deer *Capreolus capreolus*, an inhabitant of young plantations and woodland thicket and scrub, is spreading into Cornwall. Naturalists following trails established by the Forestry Commission (Details of location are given in the section *Nature reserves and other places to visit*), in Neroche Forest and Eggesford Forest stand very good chances of seeing this attractive small deer, as do those visiting such other places as Long Wood reserve, Lickham Common, Ashculm Turbary and Axmouth–Lyme Regis Undercliffs National Nature Reserve.

Normally roe deer enjoy a varied diet, feeding on leaves of brambles, trees and small plants. Their grazing and browsing can have adverse effects on forestry but the most prominent type of damage occurs when the bucks fray stems with their antlers, removing the bark so that young saplings are deformed or destroyed.

Regarded as a harmless introduction, the muntjac (or barking deer) *Muntiacus reevesi* has appeared in the West Country in recent years. A small species living in dense cover, it may well be more abundant and widespread than present records suggest. Much remains to be discovered about the life and habits of muntjac in the wild, and it is hoped that observation of a pair introduced on to Steep Holm may provide some interesting information.

The habits of the feral goats *Capra* (domestic) of Lundy have certainly fascinated students of animal behaviour, one of whom has produced a diagram of 'a hierarchy of startle reactions'. Descended from domestic goats abandoned when people left the island as the quarries declined, the animals are thoroughly adapted to life on steep rocks and cliff faces. In recent years people have once again influenced the status of the goats of Lundy by severely culling the herd.

The ponies of Dartmoor and Exmoor live in a semi-wild state. There is no evidence to support the suggestion that they are directly descended from indigenous wild horses. Experts consider that they are more likely to be descended from domesticated stock brought to this country since the New Stone Age or Neolithic. Like sheep and cattle, which people also turn out to graze on West Country moors, ponies affect the growth of vegetation, eating plants that are palatable to them, leaving others. Their habit of rubbing against tree trunks and rocks may prevent such surfaces from being colonized by lichens and mosses, and, of course, the gnawing of bark may damage or kill saplings and even larger trees and shrubs.

Man, potentially the most dangerous and most destructive of all creatures, affects other mammals (and not only mammals) in many different ways, some already mentioned. He releases or permits the escape of such introduced species as mink, grey squirrel and certain deer. He destroys many mammals as pests or vermin. He kills other in the interest of sport or financial gain and, as in the case of the Lundy goats, decides that some species need controlling not only in the interest of agriculture, horticulture or forestry but of the animals themselves (badly injured and diseased individuals *are* often removed in this way).

On occasion he destroys the habitats of animals or seriously modifies them, sometimes without good reason. All this happens or has happened in the West Country, as elsewhere, but the picture is not entirely one of unrelieved gloom or blackness. For certain species have been given legal protection, otter havens are being established along some rivers, and more areas are being set aside as nature reserves. One can only conclude this chapter by appealing to readers with a special interest in mammals to do all they can to support such bodies as the British Deer Society and the Otter Trust and others concerned with the interests of our British mammals.

Breeding Birds

Scientific names of birds mentioned here are given in the *Index of West Country Birds* (pp. 132–140), where the reader will find brief notes on most species recorded for the region, including many not referred to in this chapter.

SEA-BIRDS

Fulmars nest on cliffs along the coasts and on Lundy and the Isles of Scilly. These magnificent gliders feed on oily offal and surface plankton, including many jelly-fish. They spend some time wandering across northern seas, but from about December until mid-September they are present on the breeding cliffs, where laying takes place in May or June. Broken eggs and those taken by gulls are not replaced, a serious matter for a species which normally lays only a single egg.

Manx shearwaters breed on Annet, an uninhabited island in the Isles of Scilly, and there is a small colony on Lundy. When these long-winged birds are not at sea, catching small fish, they spend the day in their nest-burrows, departing and returning at night. Even so, they are not always able to avoid the attacks of great black-backed gulls. Manx shearwaters usually leave for southern waters during September and start to return to the breeding grounds about February.

Once described as 'like a marine house martin', the storm petrel, the smallest British sea-bird, breeds on Annet, Gulland Rock (off the north coast of Cornwall) and probably in several other uninhabited or relatively inaccessible places. From April to September–October it spends the daylight hours in the nest chamber, an earth burrow or rock crevice, or at sea, searching for surface plankton and small fish. After the breeding season the storm-finch (to use an old Cornish name) sojourns in home waters before leaving to spend the winter in the open Atlantic. Like several other species, it suffers heavy predation by great black-backed gulls.

Shags, sea-birds that feed mainly in deeper water.

The lesser black-backed gull, which (as seen here) usually nests on the ground, is a successful predator and scavenger.

Large and conspicuous as they stand with outstretched wings, cormorants nest in colonies on cliff ledges, sea stacks and islets along the north and south coasts, on Steep Holm and the Isles of Scilly, and are present at these breeding-places from late March until mid-September. Fishing in shallow coastal waters, estuaries and suitable inland waters, they have on occasion been persecuted by fishermen because of the flatfish and other saleable varieties taken. Shags, smaller birds than cormorants, feed mainly in deeper water, taking such fish as sand-eels and sprats. They breed along coasts of the mainland (more commonly on the Cornish stretches) and those of Lundy and some islands in Scilly, selecting as nesting sites crevices among rocks, ledges on cliffs and others in sea-caves.

There are breeding stations of the three auks, guillemot, razorbill and puffin, on the north Cornish coast and also on Lundy and Scilly. Like razorbills, which are much less fond of open cliff ledges, guillemots sometimes nest under and between large boulders, a habit affording them a measure of protection against great black-backs and other gulls. Although they often use burrows or cavities, puffins, also victims of predatory gulls, will sometimes nest among boulders.

As already indicated, certain species of gull prey on other birds, exerting at times a severe control on their numbers. In the West Country, the great black-backed gull, the most successful predator of all the British gulls, breeds on cliff-ledges, stacks and islets along mainland coasts and on Scilly, Lundy and Steep Holm. In addition to other birds and their eggs and young, the diet of great black-backs includes offal and other types of waste, rabbits, fish and shellfish. Much the same type of food is taken by the lesser black-backed gull. This species breeds in the areas of some of the great black-backed gull's breeding stations, where it nests on the ground or even, as happened on Steep Holm, in bushes.

Kittiwakes at their breeding ledges.

Common tern, also called 'sea swallow'.

As predators, herring gulls affect auks, taking, for example, eggs and chicks of razorbills and guillemots. As klepto-parasites, they harass puffins carrying fish to their young. Common and widespread, herring gulls nest on West Country coasts and islands, on rooftops in coastal towns and in disused Cornish china-clay pits. This enterprising bird even attempted to nest in a coniferous tree near St Austell. Very much a maritime species, the kittiwake breeds on narrow ledges on precipitous sea-cliffs, notably in west Cornwall and on Scilly, Lundy and the south Devon coast. Feeding mainly on fish and crustacea, it is often harassed by larger gulls when these species have gained little from their own fishing. Black-headed gulls are abundant on estuaries and farms, especially in winter, but very few have attempted to nest in the region in recent years.

Nowadays only two species of tern, the common and the roseate, breed in our area. Their nesting sites are confined to the Isles of Scilly, where, as in several other parts of Britain, these graceful 'sea swallows' have suffered through human disturbance, the activities of gulls and rats, and the destruction of nests by high seas. Of course, terns and other sea-birds are subject to hazards additional to those already mentioned. One, oil pollution, immediately comes to mind. Its effects on guillemots, razorbills, cormorants, shags and other species are truly dreadful.

Ringed plover. Nests, such as this, were formerly found much more commonly on West Country beaches.

WADERS

Although some breeding populations have been affected by increased use and disturbance of coastal areas and reclamation and drainage of land, at least ten species of wader have nested in the West Country in recent years. A noisy and conspicuous bird, the oystercatcher breeds, often in very small numbers, along suitable stretches of coast and also on Scilly and Lundy. Sometimes nesting among stones at the foot of the cliffs, it also selects sites on the cliffs themselves and on offshore stacks. Formerly nesting much more commonly on West Country shingle beaches, the ringed plover now breeds on Scilly and at a few places on the Devon and Somerset coasts. It will nest away from the beaches on the islands, but does not appear to breed inland on the West Country mainland. A small and dainty species whose diet comprises molluscs, insects, crustaceans and worms, the ringed plover loses many nests to gulls, rats and other predators and some are washed away by high tides.

As a breeding species, the lapwing is absent from Scilly and a large stretch of west Cornwall, but it nests in most other parts of the region, enlivening moors, farmland and grazing marshes with its unmistakable call and display-flight. The lapwing's conspicuous curved crest has earned it the nickname of horniwink in the West Country, where, as elsewhere, it is recognized as a useful bird whose diet includes many insect pests. The curlew breeds on Exmoor,

Dartmoor, Bodmin Moor and the Somerset Levels and in several other parts of the West Country, but it is not known to do so in Scilly, much of west Cornwall and a number of other areas. It is well worth visiting the breeding grounds early in the year to witness the male curlew's gliding flight and to hear its trill, a crescendo of beautiful bubbling notes.

Just as fascinating is the display flight of the common snipe. This small wader was once more widespread as a West Country breeding species, but it still nests on Bodmin Moor (its main Cornish breeding centre), Exmoor, Dartmoor and the Somerset Levels and in several other wet or boggy places. Like other birds that find much of their food by probing in mud, snipe suffer badly during severe winters and periods of prolonged drought. The woodcock, another long-billed prober, nests in comparatively few parts of the West Country, and Somerset is probably its regional breeding stronghold. It is, of course, possible that nesting by this woodland species, with its crepuscular habits, is under-recorded. This may be true of the black-tailed godwit and redshank (Somerset) and the golden plover and dunlin (Dartmoor), species known to have bred in the areas indicated, and of the common sandpiper, which is suspected of having bred in Devon and Somerset in recent years.

Curlew. The male's beautiful trill enlivens the breeding grounds early in the year.

BIRDS OF PREY

The secrecy surrounding the presence and activities of certain birds of prey is usually deliberate, for they are still subject to considerable persecution, harassment and disturbance, much of it illegal. Nevertheless one can say that at least eleven species bred in the region during the past ten years and it is possible (or probable) that another two species also did so.

The peregrine, whose total European population is not likely to be more than 1,000 pairs, has bred in Devon and Cornwall in recent years, and happily this splendid falcon shows signs of recovering from its earlier marked decline. Many peregrines were officially destroyed during the Second World War, when it was feared that they would kill homing pigeons carrying vital military messages. Later the species was badly affected by the accumulation from its prey, mainly medium-sized birds, of organochlorine pesticides. Now afforded special legal protection in Great Britain, the peregrine should be allowed to live in peace and to continue recolonizing its old West Country haunts, the tall sea-cliffs from whose tops past generations admired this magnificent and matchless flier.

The red kite was exterminated as a breeding bird in England and Scotland before the end of the nineteenth century and for many years the small British breeding population has been confined to Wales. Bird-watchers who helped with the national survey organized by the British Trust for Ornithology believed, however, that the species may have bred in at least two parts of the West Country during 1968–72. They were not certain that it actually did so, and there is no news of breeding having been confirmed in the region in subsequent years. What is known for certain is that a red kite, one of a pair which had been present in the area for months, was poisoned in Somerset during 1971–2. Such an act is not only illegal but is committed in ignorance of the fact that red kites kill very few gamebirds and would be unable to attack young poultry if these were properly penned and housed. The truth is that, as predators, red kites take voles, rats and other small mammals and such birds as black-headed gulls, woodpigeons and young jackdaws, crows and magpies. As scavengers, they eat waste and carrion of various types, including dead lambs.

Montagu's harrier, our rarest diurnal bird of prey and one that is in very real danger of becoming extinct as a British breeding species, bred successfully on a Devon common in 1976. With the agreement of the landowner, members of the Royal Society for the Protection of Birds and the Devon Bird-watching and Preservation Society wardened the nesting area, and it is almost certain that without their vigilance the two young would not have survived. The voluntary wardens not only kept people away from the gorse bushes where nesting took place but prevented a roadside fire from spreading and provided food for the young when the male bird, normally the family's food-provider, went missing, never to return. The species, whose main food in the West Country is small birds and mammals, reptiles and frogs, bears the name of Colonel George Montagu, the nineteenth-century ornithologist who studied harriers in Devon.

Merlins have bred on Exmoor in recent years and possibly in a few other parts of the West Country. Important predators of small birds, their future depends to a large extent on the conservation of their moorland breeding grounds. The hobby, whose British population is believed to be about a hundred

Left
Merlin, whose future depends to a large extent on the conservation of its moorland breeding grounds.

Right
This bird, the buzzard, is seen soaring over many parts of the West Country.

Far right
Sparrowhawk, a woodland species whose main food consists of small birds.

pairs, breeds in all three counties of the region. It feeds on large insects and small birds, and often has its nests robbed by crows.

Three other diurnal birds of prey that breed in the West Country are widely distributed and quite numerous. Anyone who has watched the kestrel hovering in search of voles and other prey, even in gale-force winds, will appreciate the aptness of its popular name, windhover. Travellers on motorways will see this long-tailed falcon hunting along grassy banks and verges and it may even be observed in urban areas. Sparrowhawks, secretive birds of woodland and wooded farmland, feed mainly on small birds, also taking small mammals and insects. Buzzards, whose soaring displays are truly magnificent, favour wooded areas and may be seen over Dartmoor, Exmoor and many other parts of the region. Their diet consists mainly of rabbits, voles, wild birds, reptiles, amphibians and insects.

Four species of owl have definitely bred in the West Country during the past ten years and another, the short-eared owl, has probably done so, too. The barn owl selects as nesting sites isolated old trees, buildings and ruins, in whose neighbourhood it may be seen hunting at dusk. Widely distributed and beneficial, it feeds on voles, shrews and mice. The tawny owl is a widespread woodland species that also frequents farmland and built-up areas. Eating many small mammals, it also takes small birds and earthworms, and may be seen catching moths and other insects. With a somewhat patchy distribution pattern in the

West Country, the little owl, an introduced species, occurs in open country and urban areas, its haunts including waste ground and old quarries, sea-cliffs and sand-dunes. Its diet comprises small mammals and birds, and earthworms, snails, beetles and other invertebrates. The long-eared owl has bred in Devon and Somerset in recent years, but is undoubtedly scarce in the region. Sadly owls suffer from illegal persecution on occasion and many are killed on main roads.

WATERFOWL

A familiar bird of the waterside, the heron breeds in many parts of the region, usually nesting in trees, though a few cases of cliff-nesting have occurred. With a diet that includes fish, frogs, water voles and young water-birds, it may at times exert a strong control on the populations of certain of its food species. The heron itself suffers badly during severe winters. Gales sometimes bring down trees bearing nests containing eggs and young, and the felling of trees also causes problems for the species.

The bittern, a secretive inhabitant of dense reedbeds that eats much the same type of food as the heron, has bred in Somerset, and one hopes that every effort will be made to ensure its freedom from disturbance. The mute swan is usually left undisturbed, but people do occasionally damage its nests and also kill cygnets. This large and stately bird breeds on ponds, lakes and rivers, and is

Little owl, an introduced species, whose haunts include open country and urban areas.

Mallard, an abundant and widespread West Country breeding duck.

particularly well distributed throughout Somerset. Farmers in that county have complained of the presence of swans on grazing meadows, and there is no doubt that they are wasteful feeders that can cause damage by trampling, fouling and tearing up plants by the roots.

Similar complaints have been made about the damage to grazing and crops by the Canada goose. A North American species, this handsome bird now breeds on lakes and reservoirs in Devon and Somerset. Members of a small flock at Enmore Park Lake, Somerset, have, according to local newspapers, regularly retrieved golf-balls from the water. This was not, of course, the reason why, in 1949, such an ornamental species was introduced to Shobrooke Park, Devon, a centre from which it has since spread. Colourful and goose-like, the shelduck breeds on Scilly and at many points at or near the region's mainland coast, especially along the southern part. Nesting mainly in burrows, often old rabbit holes, in sand-dunes, on sandy cliff-tops and in woodland banks and railway embankments, it is also called the burrow-duck. With a mixed diet, including both plant and animal foods, the shelduck feeds in sandy and muddy places.

The mallard is the most abundant and widespread of the remaining West Country breeding ducks, its nests being found at many types of site on Scilly and Lundy and in most parts of the mainland. Mallard are often hand-reared and released by wildfowlers and, to complicate the picture even more, wild mallard drakes will, given the chance, breed with farmyard ducks. Mallard eat corn, acorns and many types of plant, earthworms, crustaceans, insects and small fish. Their numbers are controlled by man and by such other species as mink, fox and pike.

Although it does nest in Somerset and Devon and on Scilly, the shoveler, unmistakable with its enormous spatulate bill, is absent as a breeding species from a large part of the region. On Devon marshes, ducklings of this species have been attacked by short-eared owls, and there have been cases of eggs being destroyed by cattle trampling the lined hollows that serve as nests. The teal nests in thick cover and tries hard to keep its young out of sight, and it is often difficult to locate its breeding sites. We know, however, that this tiny duck does nest on Scilly and that it is thinly distributed as a breeding species on the West Country mainland.

Gadwalls breed on Scilly and in a few parts of Somerset, where their nests are hidden in thick vegetation, usually in quiet spots close to the water. In recent years both the garganey and the pochard have nested at a few places in Somerset and possibly at one or two other West Country sites. The tufted duck has bred on lakes and reservoirs in Somerset and may also have nested in other parts of the region. Feeding mainly on small forms of animal life, it is very fond of the introduced zebra mussel.

Adorned with ear tufts and crest, the great crested grebe is an attractive member of the West Country fauna. Most of its breeding sites are on lakes, pits and reservoirs in Somerset, but young are also reared annually at Slapton Ley in Devon. The striped nestlings gain a measure of protection against pike and other predators by riding on the backs of their parents. Expert divers, great crested grebes eat mostly insects and fish. A smaller bird, the little grebe or dabchick is more widespread as a West Country breeding species, though there are large parts of Devon where it does not appear to nest.

RAILS AND CRAKES

Widely distributed as a breeding species on the West Country mainland, but usually avoiding the higher stretches of moorland, the moorhen also nests on Scilly. Any freshwater habitat, whether it be pond or lake, reservoir or river, is likely to attract it. The bird's food consists mainly of vegetable matter, but about a quarter is made up of worms, insects and other small animals. In autumn and winter moorhens may be seen eating berries in the branches of hawthorn bushes and feeding on fallen apples in orchards and gardens. They have also been known to take oatmeal, fat and other foods from bird-tables. On Tresco, Isles of Scilly, they have dug up and eaten potatoes, causing significant damage.

Our largest British rail, the coot, eats large amounts of grass and weeds, supplementing its diet with molluscs, insects, worms and small fish. Breeding on Scilly and many parts of the mainland, the coot prefers larger stretches of water than the moorhen, a more densely distributed species. The water rail nests in reedbeds and other dense waterside vegetation in comparatively few West Country localities. Somewhat elusive in the breeding season, it will often venture into the open in winter, when individuals may even be seen feeding in gardens, occasionally under bird-tables.

Thinly and patchily distributed as a West Country breeding species, the corncrake nests in hayfields, where young have been killed in recent years by grass-cutting machines and dogs. A very difficult species to locate, the spotted crake may breed in one or two places in the region.

Moorhen, a species that favours freshwater habitats of many kinds.

GAME BIRDS

The commonest and most widespread game bird breeding in the West Country is the pheasant, an introduced alien whose presence in Scilly and certain other parts has been strengthened by the release of birds for sporting purposes. Often thought of as shy, wary and very suspicious of man, its worst predator, the pheasant will nevertheless nest in gardens, though its more usual nesting-place is on the ground in woods, hedgerows and reedbeds. Generally the species, one that eats vast quantities of wireworms, is beneficial to agriculture, but individuals may be harmful, as when they consume large amounts of grain. Pheasants may exert a strong local control on the numbers of some animal species, as is obvious from the fact that a cock bird once had eight baby adders in its crop.

Also breeding in most parts of the region, the grey partridge, our native species, prefers agricultural land and usually avoids the high ground of areas such as Dartmoor and Exmoor. The introduced red-legged partridge, whose numbers are boosted from time to time by the release of birds from game-farms, occurs as a breeding species in Somerset and east Devon. Somewhat like a tiny partridge, the quail is a summer visitor to Britain, arriving from Africa in May or June and departing in September or October. Breeding on Scilly and in scattered West Country localities, it nests in growing corn or mowing grass, where its eggs and young are sometimes disturbed and even destroyed during farming operations. More plentiful in 'quail years' than at other times, the bird, one renowned for its clear, musical 'wet-mi'lips' call, is more often heard than seen. Young of the bob-white quail, an American species, were first released on Tresco, Isles of Scilly, where a breeding population has been established, in 1964.

Two species of grouse, the black and the red, breed in Somerset and Devon.

The turtle dove, a summer visitor to Britain, winters mainly in Africa. As seen here, the nest is a slight platform of twigs.

The black grouse, a bird of moorland and birch and conifer woods, lives on Exmoor, where hand-reared birds have been released to reinforce the population, Dartmoor and the Quantocks. Feeding mainly on heather, black grouse will also eat buds and young shoots of trees and shrubs, grasses, herbs and insects. Lately there have been fewer West Country breeding records for the black grouse than for the red grouse. The last-named species, one inhabiting open heather moorland, was successfully introduced to Exmoor and Dartmoor during the First World War. Like black grouse, red grouse rely heavily on heather for food, the young shoots, buds, flowers and seed-heads all being taken. Herbs and berry-bearing shrubs also serve as foodplants, and insects and spiders are enjoyed by the young.

PIGEONS

The woodpigeon, a most successful bird, is common and widespread, its West Country breeding stations including Scilly, Lundy and Steep Holm. Feeding, often greedily, on many kinds of plant food, it can be harmful to agriculture, a fact well established in the region, where fields of kale and cabbage have been stripped in winter. Feral pigeons, whose wild ancestors, rock doves, once bred on West Country cliffs, nest on buildings and ruins in many places. Stock doves colonized the West Country about a century ago, and now breed in most parts, nesting in holes in trees, cliffs and quarries.

A summer visitor that winters mainly in Africa, the turtle dove is associated with arable farmland and other habitats of fumitory, one of its favourite foodplants. It is a scarce breeding species in Cornwall but quite abundant in Somerset and Devon. Much more widely distributed as a West Country breeding bird than the turtle dove, the collared dove is attracted to farms, chicken runs and other places where grain is likely to be available. A species of both town and country, the collared dove has colonized Britain in a remarkable way since it first nested here in 1955.

WOODPECKERS

The green woodpecker, the largest woodpecker nesting in Britain, breeds in most parts of the region, its loud cry or 'yaffle' being a familiar sound. A colourful species, it nests in holes in mature trees and feeds largely on ants. The great spotted woodpecker, another widespread West Country breeding species, is more closely associated with woodland than the green woodpecker, whose habitats are stretches of farmland, parkland and dry heathland where mature trees are present. The great spotted woodpecker, a frequent visitor to bird tables in the region, eats insects and their larvae, fruit and seeds, and eggs and young of small birds. An insect-eater, the lesser spotted woodpecker usually keeps to the tree-tops. This habit and its smallness (it is about the size of a house sparrow) often enable it to escape detection, but breeding has nevertheless been confirmed in many West Country localities.

HOOPOE

Like woodpeckers, the hoopoe, unmistakable with its tall, long crest and long, down-curved bill, usually nests in holes in trees. A casual breeder in this country,

Kingfisher, a colourful 'feathered fisherman'.

The loud cry or 'yaffle' of this bird, the green woodpecker, is a familiar sound in most parts of the region.

it has nested in Cornwall and Somerset in recent years. Although the hoopoe is afforded special legal protection here, details of the locations of its breeding sites are, quite rightly, not broadcast. Grasshoppers, crickets and other insects and small lizards form its main food items.

KINGFISHER

Kingfishers nest in horizontal tunnels in waterside banks along many streams and rivers. These colourful 'feathered fishermen' eat small fishes, insects and water-snails, and are not averse to fishing in garden ponds in towns or in rock pools at the coast. They are badly affected by hard winters, river pollution and disturbance of their nesting sites.

CUCKOO AND 'CUCKOO'S MATE'

The 'cuckoo's mate', the wryneck, is now an extremely scarce migrant breeder in Britain, but there have been a few suggestions that the species may have bred in orchards in Devon and Somerset during the past few years. The cuckoo itself, a much more abundant and widespread migrant breeder, lays its eggs in the nests of dunnocks, meadow pipits, reed warblers and other hosts. In defence of this parasite, one can only say that it eats large numbers of insect pests and that its familiar call-note does add something to the atmosphere of the countryside.

SWIFT

Much the same could be said of the swift, a common and widely distributed summer visitor that rushes through the air, uttering a penetrating scream and feeding on flying insects of many kinds. Although swifts mainly nest under eaves, nest-boxes provided on the church tower at Dartington in Devon are used successfully by this mobile species.

NIGHTJAR

We cannot pass on to the birds of the great order Passeriformes without mentioning the nightjar. Crepuscular, nocturnal and insect-eating, this summer visitor breeds on West Country heaths and moors, and has even been known to nest on Porlock beach. With its weird churring song, it is more often heard than seen.

LARKS

The skylark, the most widely distributed bird in Britain and Ireland, breeds on Scilly and Lundy and throughout the West Country mainland. A species of open country, it enlivens moors and meadows, fields and dunes, the male giving its beautiful song as it mounts high into the sky. This much-admired songster eats many insects, but it becomes something of an agricultural pest when grazing seedling crops. The woodlark, a declining species, is much more thinly distributed, but the region is one of its breeding strongholds in Britain. The male's rich song is heard in such places as heaths and commons, where the species seeks insects among the short grass of close-cropped ground.

SWALLOW AND MARTINS

Breeding throughout the West Country, including Scilly and Lundy, that familiar summer visitor the swallow builds its mud nest on beams and ledges in farm buildings, garages, sheds and even houses. An aerial feeder, it takes insects, some of them distributed by grazing animals whose pastures are among the bird's favourite haunts. Another common and widely distributed summer resident, the house martin builds most of its nests under the eaves of houses, though cliff nesting also occurs. A more local breeding species, the sand martin nests in burrows in sand-pits, river banks and cliffs. Like swallows, martins are insect-eaters.

WAGTAILS

Equally at home in farmyard and suburban situation, the pied wagtail is widespread as a West Country breeding bird. A graceful species with lively dancing movements, it nests in holes and other well hidden places, a partly covered engine top having been used in Devon. It is difficult to believe that this insect-eater could ever be regarded as a nuisance, but this is exactly what it does become when roosting in greenhouses in large numbers. Elegant and attractive, the grey wagtail nests near or above fast-flowing stretches of streams and rivers in many parts of the region. With a fondness for low-lying grazing meadows, the yellow wagtail has its main West Country breeding sites in Somerset and along the south Devon coast.

Meadow pipit, a common host to the cuckoo.

PIPITS

An insect-eater with the characteristic call 'peep-peep-peep', the meadow pipit breeds on commons, rough grassland and moorland, including some of the highest parts of Dartmoor and Exmoor. Widespread and abundant it often falls victim to birds of prey and is, as already mentioned, a common host to the cuckoo. As a breeding species, the tree pipit is scarce in west Cornwall and some other parts of the region, but there are many nesting sites on heaths, commons and stretches of moorland, where scattered bushes or trees serve as song-posts for the males. The rock pipit breeds on Scilly and Lundy and along the rocky shores of the mainland. Like the meadow pipit, it is a common host of the cuckoo.

RED-BACKED SHRIKE

The red-backed shrike, a bird with the habit of impaling insects and other small animals on thorns, has been declining in Britain for many years. Not surprisingly, therefore, it is now a very scarce and irregular breeder in the West Country.

DIPPER

Continually bobbing, the dipper occurs on fast-running rivers and streams, nesting by the water, beside and behind waterfalls and under bridges. Abundant and widespread in Devon, serving as the emblem of that county's nature conservation trust, it also breeds in Somerset and Cornwall. The dipper, whose diet comprises insects, larvae of insects and amphibians, crustaceans, molluscs, worms and fish and their eggs, is an accomplished underwater feeder. It has even been known to feed under ice, though it can suffer very badly during severe winters.

The dipper, emblem of the Devon Trust for Nature Conservation.

WREN

The wren can also be severely affected by such conditions. Fortunately this adaptable little bird has always managed to recover from its misfortunes, and may well have become the commonest nesting species in Britain and Ireland. In the region it breeds on Scilly and Lundy and throughout the mainland, nesting in most kinds of habitat. In Devon a pair built their nest behind the rear wheel of a Land Rover! Although the species feeds mainly on insects and spiders, wrens entered the closed area of a trout hatchery and took newly hatched fry from a tank.

DUNNOCK

Busy, yet unobtrusive, the dunnock or hedge sparrow is a common West Country breeding bird, nesting on Scilly and Lundy and in almost every part of the mainland. Often thought to be dull, it is, in fact, a quietly attractive bird, whose song is not without its individual charm. It is an important host to the cuckoo.

ROBIN

Like the dunnock, the robin, Britain's national bird, is abundant and widely distributed, nesting in a wide variety of habitats, including hedges, gardens and moorland conifer plantations. It takes many kinds of insects, being particularly fond of small beetles and caterpillars, and also feeds on spiders, earthworms, small molluscs, seeds and berries. In winter, as every bird-lover knows, the robin visits bird-tables and occasionally enters houses. Cats kill many robins in some areas, but the species is also attacked by birds of prey and other enemies. It seems appropriate to mention that many of Dr David Lack's classic studies on the robin were carried out at Dartington in Devon (see his book, *The Life of the Robin*).

NIGHTINGALE

As a West Country breeding bird, the nightingale is confined to Somerset and east Devon. The national survey of 1976 showed that the species is declining and that Devon is an area where it has shown a distinct contraction of range. A celebrated songster, the nightingale is attracted to dense thickets, woods with thick undergrowth and overgrown hedges, and it is feared that the continued removal of scrub in the interests of peat extraction will severely reduce the amount of suitable habitat in Somerset.

REDSTART

The redstart breeds in all three counties of the region. An adaptable species of mature woodland and parkland, it nests in holes, often in trees or walls. Its old name of firetail suits this insect-eating summer visitor with the constantly flicking reddish-orange tail.

CHATS

The whinchat breeds on moors, heaths and commons and in other rough gorsy places in Somerset and Devon and on Bodmin Moor in Cornwall. Like many other species (including mammals, insects and plants), it suffers from loss

Whinchat, a species that has made good use of newly created forestry plantations.

Wheatear, an early summer visitor.

of habitat when tidying operations in the countryside become excessive. On the credit side, breeding whinchats make good use of newly created forestry plantations. As a West Country breeding bird, the stonechat is more widely distributed than the whinchat, its nesting areas including Scilly and many parts of Cornwall. With a strong liking for coastal districts, stonechats inhabit moors, commons and other uncultivated places where gorse and heather abound but where there are short grassy areas too. As far as the southern half of England is concerned, the West Country is an important breeding stronghold for this conspicuous chat, whose distinctive call is like two stones being knocked together.

WHEATEAR

Nesting in holes in the ground (rabbit burrows are a favourite site), walls, ruins and rocks, the wheatear breeds on Dartmoor, Exmoor and Bodmin Moor and in several other parts of the region, many of them on the coast. One of the first summer visitors to arrive in Britain, it feeds on small beetles, larvae of flies and other small invertebrates, thriving where the turf is kept very short by grazing animals.

BLACKBIRD AND RING OUZEL

The blackbird, whose song is so beautifully rich and fluted, is an abundant breeding species throughout the West Country, the islands included. Originally a woodland bird, it now nests in many kinds of situation, both rural and urban, avoiding only the very highest stretches of open moorland. The blackbird feeds mostly on worms, insects and other small forms of animal life in summer, taking fruits, berries and seeds in winter. In Devon, during the very dry summer of 1976, however, blackbirds were seen feeding their young on berries. Looking somewhat like a blackbird with a crescent of white (off-white in the female) on the breast, the ring ouzel is a comparatively scarce breeder on the higher and more isolated parts of Dartmoor, Exmoor and Bodmin Moor.

THRUSHES

Fairly common and widespread, the song thrush usually nests in bushes or low trees, but sometimes does so on the ground and in other situations. Well known for its delightful song with oft-repeated phrases, it is not as numerous or as enterprising as the blackbird. Though it also feeds on spiders and insects and fruits and berries in season, the song thrush eats many snails and earthworms. These items also form part of the diet of the mistle thrush, the largest British thrush. Common and widely distributed in the West Country, it nests in woods and plantations, hedgerow trees, large gardens and town parks, parts of Dartmoor, Exmoor and Bodmin Moor being among its breeding grounds. Bold and hardy, the mistle thrush continues to sing loudly during gales (hence its local name of storm-cock) and angrily drives away predators.

WARBLERS

With its distinctive two-note song, the chiffchaff is well known in most parts of the region. Nesting in low undergrowth, it breeds in woods and suitable

Ring ouzels photographed on Exmoor.

gardens and on commons and heaths. Generally the chiffchaff is a summer visitor, but some individuals remain here throughout the winter. Their favourite wintering sites include sewage farms in west Cornwall, where on occasion large numbers have been found on the filter beds. The blackcap is another widely distributed migrant breeder, small numbers of which stay here and visit bird tables in winter. It nests in large gardens, thorn scrub and woods with thick undergrowth, and eats such berries as those of ivy, mistletoe and cotoneaster when insects are not available.

Despite the crash in breeding numbers of 1969, the whitethroat still nests in the cover of brambles, nettles and scrub on many West Country sites, some fairly high on moorland. The lesser whitethroat, a much scarcer bird, appears to breed mainly in Somerset and east Devon. A common and widely distributed summer visitor, the willow warbler nests in open woods and bushy places, and is often confused with the chiffchaff when it is not singing. The new conifer plantations on Bodmin Moor and elsewhere and other places with overgrown, tangled vegetation make ideal breeding sites for the grasshopper warbler, a

Blackcap, a summer visitor, small numbers of which stay here in winter.

The bold and hardy mistle thrush, an early nester.

summer resident whose reeling song may be heard in many parts of the region.

The wood warbler, a locally common summer visitor, breeds in open, mature deciduous woods, including oakwoods on Dartmoor and Exmoor. Despite its name, the garden warbler, a fairly well distributed summer visitor, nests in woods and bushy places, and is one of several species that have colonized new conifer plantations on Dartmoor and elsewhere. Of the three waterside warblers, all summer visitors, the sedge warbler is the commonest and most widespread. Breeding mostly by fresh water and in marshy places (also sometimes in drier ones), it hides its nest in dense vegetation. Nests of the reed warbler, a locally distributed West Country breeding species, are much more conspicuous, most of them being attached to stems of the common reed. The marsh warbler is very scarce and very local in England, but a few pairs have nested in Somerset in recent years.

The Dartford warbler, a very scarce species of heaths and gorsy commons, has nested in Devon during the past few years. This is a pleasing state of affairs and one hopes that this delightful bird, a resident that has suffered badly as the result of heath fires and severe winters, will be allowed to continue strengthening its numbers in the West Country. Another exciting ornithological event occurred when Cetti's warbler bred in south Devon in 1975, three years after breeding was first confirmed in Britain. A resident species feeding on insects, Cetti's warbler is, like the Dartford warbler, badly affected by severe weather.

GOLDCREST

Another species whose population crashes in hard weather is the goldcrest. Locally common on Scilly, Lundy and the mainland, our smallest European bird prefers to nest in conifers, taking readily to exotic species introduced

A summer visitor, the pied flycatcher is attracted to old oak woodland.

during afforestation. Suspended hammockwise on the outer ends of branches, the nests are safe from most predators, but agile grey squirrels often manage to reach and rob them. The goldcrest's normal diet comprises small insects and spiders, items that are supplemented in severe winters by food taken from bird tables.

FLYCATCHERS

A summer visitor, the spotted flycatcher occurs on Scilly and throughout the mainland. Breeding fairly commonly in churchyards and farmyards, parks and gardens, orchards and woodland edges, this alert species stations itself at its look-out post, a branch or fence perhaps, ready to dash out and capture any insect that flies past. Another summer visitor, but a much more localized one, the pied flycatcher breeds on Dartmoor and Exmoor and in several other West Country localities. It is attracted to oak woodland where old trees provide holes for nesting and where there is adequate food in the form of defoliating caterpillars. Yarner Wood, Devon, is one place where the provision of nest-boxes has encouraged pied flycatchers to breed.

TITMICE

The erection of nest-boxes has also brought increased numbers of blue tits into woods, plantations, hedgerows and gardens where natural nesting holes are in short supply. The blue tit, Britain's most widely distributed and most abundant

This long-tailed tit has just returned to its nest with food. Like other insect-eaters, it suffers badly in hard weather.

tit, breeds in every suitable part of the West Country, including the Isles of Scilly, using both natural and man-made sites. People may grumble when the species damages fruit or opens milk-bottles, but it is important to remember that it destroys large numbers of insect pests.

Another abundant resident, whose general West Country distribution pattern resembles that of the blue tit, the great tit also makes use of nest-boxes. The coal tit will nest in boxes, but it rears many broods in holes in the ground and crevices in walls. Common and widespread, it favours conifer plantations. Despite the impression given by its name, the marsh tit, a widely but often thinly distributed resident, inhabits deciduous woods and certain other places with trees, nesting in holes, both natural and artificial. The willow tit is often confused with the marsh tit, and it may well be more widespread as a West Country breeding species than existing records suggest. Breeding in mixed deciduous woods and places with scattered trees, the willow tit excavates its nest hole in soft, rotten wood. Quiet and undemonstrative for a tit, and not separated from the marsh tit in Britain until 1900, it clearly deserves further study.

Unlike other British titmice, the long-tailed tit is not a hole-nester. This widespread species builds its nest, a ball of moss, cobwebs and hair, decorated with fragments of lichens and lined with countless feathers, in bushes in overgrown and scrubby places. A very small insect-eater, the long-tailed tit suffers badly in hard weather, but, like several other tits, it will feed at bird tables in winter.

NUTHATCH AND TREECREEPER

A hole-nesting species of woodland and other places with mature trees, the nuthatch breeds in many parts of the region. Insects and larvae are taken as it climbs up and down tree-trunks, and the bird also feeds on hazel nuts, beech-mast and acorns, wedging them in crevices in bark and using its bill to open them. One day in May, Cornish nuthatches were seen collecting pieces of bread from a roadside picnic site and storing them behind the loose bark of a tree trunk. The treecreeper, another widely distributed species associated with trees, creeps up tree trunks in search of insects, its principal food. Its nest is usually built behind loose bark or in a crack or crevice. Unlike the nuthatch, the treecreeper uses its tail in climbing and it very rarely creeps down tree trunks.

BUNTINGS

The widely distributed yellowhammer (or yellow bunting) inhabits open country, nesting in banks, bushes and hedges. Its diet includes insects and their larvae, spiders, corn, weed seeds and wild fruits, especially blackberries. Certain of the drier habitats favoured by the yellowhammer are being occupied by the reed bunting, a bird once regarded as belonging strictly to reedbeds and other wet areas. In addition to foods similar to those of the yellowhammer, the reed bunting, a fairly widespread West Country breeder, enjoys small molluscs and crustacea.

First discovered as a British breeding species in Devon in 1800, the cirl bunting breeds locally in the West Country, one of its very few British breeding

Cirl bunting, a species that likes coastal localities and well-timbered river valleys.

strongholds, showing a liking for coastal localities and well-timbered river valleys. A Mediterranean type, enjoying warm, sheltered places, this attractive bird is badly affected by harsh weather. Though far more widely distributed and much more abundant in Britain as a whole, the corn bunting tends to avoid upland areas and is absent from a large part of the region. Nesting in rank vegetation, brambles and bushes, it breeds mainly in Somerset and along the Cornish coast.

FINCHES

The cheerful 'pink' call-note of the chaffinch is heard on Scilly and Lundy and in all parts of the West Country mainland. For this common species breeds in both rural and urban situations where trees or bushes are present. In the breeding season the chaffinch takes large numbers of insects, spiders and earthworm cocoons, and rears its young on these items. At other times it eats mainly seeds, fallen beech mast, corn and weed seeds all being enjoyed.

Abundant and widespread, the greenfinch nests in woodland fringes and young plantations, tall hedges, thickets and bushy gardens. The species, whose young are fed partly on insects and spiders, consumes vast numbers of seeds, including those of cereal crops, yew and burdock. In winter many greenfinches move into villages and towns and visit bird tables. Peanuts are eaten there, the birds clinging to containers to get at them, and a supply of pinhead oatmeal certainly attracts the species.

Widely distributed and aptly called 'the seven-coloured linnet', the goldfinch breeds in orchards, large gardens and other places with scattered trees, its deep, lichen-decorated nest often being built high on a bough. Although it does eat insects and seeds of such trees as alder and birch, this lively bird is particularly fond of seeds of thistles, dandelions, burdocks and other plants in the family Compositae.

The siskin, whose male is our yellowest finch, frequents bird tables in Exeter, Plymouth and elsewhere in winter. As a West Country breeding bird, however, it appears to be confined to conifer plantations in Devon where, in 1957, nesting was first proved on Dartmoor. Seeds of spruce, pine, birch and a few other trees are eaten, as are those of smaller plants such as dandelions and thistles.

A common and widespread species, the lively linnet nests in hedges, bushes and other low vegetation on gorsy commons, farmland and rough ground. It takes few tree seeds, depending largely on seeds of weeds of cultivation and of other wild plants. As a breeding species, the redpoll is locally distributed in the region, its nesting sites including young conifers, tall bushes and beech hedges on Exmoor, Bodmin Moor and Dartmoor. Birch seeds are an important food of this species, but seeds of alder and a number of smaller plants and insects from the opening buds of trees are also eaten.

Generally regarded as an uncommon and irregular breeder in the West Country, the hawfinch, which has been described as shy, unapproachable and elusive, may sometimes escape detection. The bullfinch, another large and handsome species, is common and widespread, nesting in overgrown hedges, bushy gardens and thickets. Given the chance, this bird, the only finch of economic importance in Britain, eats flower-buds and occasionally leaf-buds of fruit frees. Its diet also includes buds and flowers of several other trees and shrubs, seeds of ash, birch, elm and smaller plants, and various soft fruits. Spiders, caterpillars and the softer parts of seeds and small snails are fed to the young. Crossbills nest, perhaps irregularly, at a number of sites in Devon, and it is possible that larger numbers will do so in the region as more conifers produce seeds, the favourite food of these birds.

SPARROWS

Adaptable, successful and very common, house sparrows are seen in most places where there is human habitation. Often ignored by bird-watchers, they

Seen here at a nest high in a tree, the raven also breeds on cliffs and in quarries.

nevertheless make their presence felt at times. Their attacks on standing corn crops can be damaging. They annoy growers by removing buds from gooseberry bushes and certain ornamental shrubs and by attacking flowers of crocus and several other plants. Their pestering of house martins, whose nests they sometimes take over, disturbs a perfectly harmless, indeed beneficial, species. On the other hand, one must agree that house sparrows eat many weed seeds and insect pests (watch them picking aphids off rose bushes!), and their useful scavenging activities cannot be overlooked.

The tree sparrow is a much less common species in the West Country. Typically a hole-nester, it breeds, not always regularly, in Somerset and at several Devon localities. It may sometimes be overlooked, but the region is on the south-western fringes of its main British breeding area.

STARLING

Like the house sparrow, the starling breeds throughout the region, the islands included. A grassland feeder, it destroys large numbers of leatherjackets, also eating earthworms, beetles, spiders and small snails. When these animal foods are in short supply or unobtainable, starlings turn to grain and seeds of wild plants, elderberries and other fruits, food put out for poultry and livestock and household scraps. Starlings are attacked by sparrowhawks, owls, kestrels and other predators, but their numbers remain high.

CROWS

The jay inhabits woods, parks and large gardens, nesting in undergrowth and other thick cover. A noisy bird, it is widespread and common in many parts of the region. Caterpillars and other insects, acorns, soft fruits (including cultivated varieties) and eggs and young of game-birds and song-birds all form part of its diet. In some West Country areas jays are regular visitors to bird tables in gardens, where they are seen feeding from nut bags.

Like the jay, the magpie eats young birds and eggs, also taking insects, small mammals, grain and fruits. Widespread and numerous, this conspicuous, long-tailed species nests, occasionally near houses, in thorn bushes, thickets and isolated trees in a variety of habitats. Some West Country magpies visit bird tables. Others supplement their diet by picking ticks from the backs of livestock.

They share this habit with the jackdaw, a common and gregarious species that nests in holes and crevices in coastal cliffs, old trees, buildings, ruins and quarries. 'Saucy Jack', as the bird has been called from its manner and its high-pitched call-note 'tchack', consumes many insect larvae and spiders, creatures collected from grassland and the foliage of trees. It also enjoys young birds and eggs, worms, fruit and several other animal and vegetable foods. The jackdaw occasionally makes a nuisance of itself by building its nest of sticks in a chimney or a church tower, but many a countryman has a soft spot for this agile and sprightly bird.

Feelings concerning the rook are often mixed. However, despite the fact that its diet includes not only insects and carrion but cereals and potatoes, it is, on balance, a beneficial species. In the region, where nests occur in both deciduous and evergreen trees, the rook is widely distributed and abundant. As in other parts of Britain, rooks have often nested in elms in the West Country, and the destruction of trees affected by Dutch elm disease will undoubtedly cause the dispersal of a number of their colonies.

Unlike the rook (and the jackdaw), the carrion crow is a solitary nester. Breeding throughout the region, including Scilly and Lundy, it nests in trees and bushes in both rural and urban situations. As its name suggests, this all-black crow spends much time as a scavenger, feeding on the remains of creatures killed on the roads and on other forms of carrion. The bird's diet also includes many other foods, animal and vegetable, eggs and young birds being important items in some places.

The raven, another widely distributed West Country breeder, nests on coastal cliffs and in tall trees and quarries. Like the carrion crow, it eats both animal (including carrion) and vegetable foods. Sadly, the chough no longer nests in the West Country, and one must travel many miles to see this charming, red-billed and red-legged crow breeding in its natural surroundings.

Amphibians and Reptiles

Britain is not rich in the number of its kinds of amphibians and reptiles, but most of them do occur in the West Country. The three British species of newts, the warty (or great crested), the smooth and the palmate, are known in the region, and there are places (Axmouth–Lyme Regis Undercliffs National Nature Reserve is one) where all three have been recorded.

The warty newt *Triturus cristatus*, the largest of the European species, lives in fairly deep ponds and ditches in Somerset and Devon. Some individuals remain in the water all the year round, but outside the breeding season, whose duration is from about March to July, many live on land, in cracks and holes and under such cover as fallen timber and stones. The smooth newt *T. vulgaris*, the least aquatic of the British species, is locally distributed in Somerset and Devon. The palmate newt *T. helveticus*, the smallest European species, lives in all three counties of the region. Razoumowski, the Swiss naturalist, described it as a distinct species in 1788, and the first British specimens were discovered by William Baker, a West Country naturalist, in a pond at Clay Hill Farm, near Bridgwater, during the first half of the nineteenth century. Regarded as a species that prefers mountainous and hilly districts, its West Country habitats nevertheless include ponds and ditches (some brackish coastal ones) in low-lying parts.

Newts are voracious feeders, taking tadpoles, worms, insect larvae, slugs, snails and small crustacea. Their numerous enemies include fish, water-birds, hedgehogs and rats. Newt tadpoles are also attacked by certain of the larger aquatic insects and their larvae. The warty newt is perhaps more of a survivor than the other species, the distasteful secretion of its skin protecting it from at least some predators.

The common toad *Bufo bufo* is fairly abundant and widespread throughout much of the West Country. It is not familiar to everyone because it usually spends the day in a shady and sheltered place or in a hole or cavity, emerging in the late evening to hunt for food. This consists of insects (mainly ants and beetles), worms, woodlice and many other small forms of animal life. An intelligent creature (the most intelligent European amphibian, according to some experts), the toad will wait below the entrance to a hive, ready to take bees that come its way. The secretion of its skin affords a measure of protection against potential enemies, but it does not deter rats, which remove the skin before eating the flesh, crows and some snakes. Toads hibernate in holes in banks and in other dry and sheltered places from October or November until February or March. During their annual migrations to and from ponds and ditches used for spawning, many toads are killed by predators and motor traffic.

Although it is generally regarded as being absent from the counties dealt with in this book, there have been records from north Devon of the natterjack or running toad *B. calamita* in recent years. It is thought likely that these natterjacks or their parents were deliberately introduced into the region. Be this as it may, it should be noted that the natterjack is fully protected by the Conservation of Wild Creatures and Wild Plants Act 1975.

The common frog *Rana temporaria* is still widely distributed in the West Country. After spawning, an event occurring early in the year in many parts of the region, frogs leave the breeding ponds and make for damp places, where they feed on snails, slugs, beetles, larvae and other small creatures. They hibernate in mud at the bottom of ponds and ditches or in holes in waterside banks, but this resting period is brief or interrupted when, as is sometimes the case, autumn and winter are mild. Common frogs have many enemies, herons, ringed snakes, otters and rats being among the most important.

Most of the amphibians mentioned suffer from loss of habitat (the filling in of ponds, for example) and from the activities of people collecting the animals or their spawn. Ponds in nature reserves and private gardens may, therefore, serve as breeding sanctuaries for them. Any owner of a private pond who wants to get rid of spawn should contact the secretary of his local nature conservation trust who may be able to transfer it to another pond, perhaps one in a nature reserve. Gardeners can also assist the welfare of amphibians by providing some means by which they can leave steep-sided ponds. Suitably placed, a large piece of rock or a sloping plank of wood may be all that is needed.

Turning to reptiles, we reach the harmless slow-worm *Anguis fragilis* which, despite its snake-like form, is a lizard, albeit a legless one. An attractive creature with a highly polished appearance, the slow-worm occurs throughout the West Country mainland and also on Steep Holm, living in dry places, including

A pair of smooth newts (male on right) seen in the water. This species is the least aquatic of the British newts.

heaths and commons, hedgerows and roadside verges, gardens and open woods. It spends many of the daylight hours hiding beneath leaves, stones and logs and in compost heaps and loose soil, but does sometimes enjoy basking in the sun, especially in early spring and late summer.

With a diet that comprises slugs (particularly the small white ones) and snails, insects, spiders and worms, the slow-worm is often regarded as a friend by gardeners. When very young and worm-like, the blind-worm, as the slow-worm is also known, is preyed upon by frogs, toads and certain birds. Adult slow-worms have many enemies: rats, badgers, foxes, birds of prey and others. The handsome blue-spotted form of the slow-worm is also found in the West Country.

The viviparous or common lizard *Lacerta vivipara*, an agile and intelligent species, is abundant and widely distributed in the region. Between early spring and autumn it may be seen basking in the sun or heard dashing into cover on heaths, commons and sand-dunes, on banks, old walls and wasteland, and in hedgerows, gardens and open woods. Feeding mainly on spiders, insects and their larvae, it will sometimes eat worms and centipedes too. Like the slow-

Slow-worms, harmless legless lizards.

worm, the viviparous lizard is harmless and there is no reason why it should be molested in any way.

The remaining species of West Country reptiles, the ringed snake and the adder, should also be left unharmed. The golden rule is that snakes should remain unmolested at all times and should never be picked up by non-experts.

Ringed snake or grass-snake. Completely harmless, it likes to warm itself in the sun.

A pair of adders. The male (left) is normally marked, but the female is a melanic (black) specimen.

The ringed snake or grass-snake *Natrix natrix*, a non-venomous and completely harmless species, is found in all three counties of the region, though there are many parts where it is certainly not common. Living mainly in marshes, open woodlands and hedgerows, it prefers places near water where it can bask in the sunshine. Given the chance, the ringed snake feeds mainly on frogs and newts, taking fish, tadpoles and small birds and mammals at other times. A good climber and an equally proficient swimmer, it is active from about March or April (occasionally earlier) until October, when it takes refuge in a dry, sheltered hole or cavity and goes into hibernation. The females lay their eggs in June or July, depositing them in heaps of manure, rotting leaves or sawdust, where the heat of decomposition assists incubation. The young emerge six–ten weeks later and immediately go into hiding, the only way of escaping their numerous enemies. Adult ringed snakes are eaten by such mammals as badgers and hedgehogs and also by some birds of prey.

Our only poisonous British snake, the adder or viper *Vipera berus* occurs on many West Country heaths, moors, cliff-tops and sand-dunes and in woods and old mineral workings. It is quite common in some areas, and visitors to such places should wear stout boots or shoes and take the precaution of searching the ground before sitting or lying down there. An unaggressive creature that usually moves away immediately it picks up sounds conveyed by the earth, the adder will not normally attack people unless it has been stood upon, threatened or cornered. Very few deaths follow adder-bite in this country, but anyone who is bitten by this snake should be taken quickly, but quietly, to a doctor.

Adders hibernate in holes and cavities in the ground from about October until the spring. They mate in April or early May, the females giving birth to the young in August or September. Both young and adult adders are killed in large numbers by people who are often victims of fear or ignorance (or both). Other known enemies of the species include birds of prey, hedgehogs, pike and eels. The diet of the adder itself comprises nestling birds and small mammals, amphibians and reptiles. Black adders, melanic specimens of the adder, are occasionally seen in the West Country, sometimes in company with individuals marked with the normal zig-zag pattern.

The sand lizard *Lacerta agilis* and the smooth snake *Coronella austriaca*, both protected by the Conservation of Wild Creatures and Wild Plants Act 1975, do not now appear to be members of the fauna of our three counties. Naturalists should, however, keep a sharp look-out for them, as they have been recorded from the region.

Strandings of marine turtles, species outside the scope of this book, should be reported to coastguard officers so that they may inform the British Museum (Natural History) of the occurrence of these stragglers from tropical and subtropical seas.

Butterflies

Many butterflies still thrive in the West Country, most of the native British species occurring there. Several of the Pieridae, a very large family, are commonly seen, their white or yellow wings making them conspicuous in most situations. Abundant and widespread, the large and small whites, *Pieris brassicae** and *P. rapae*, are familiar to gardeners and many other people. Their larvae eat such cultivated plants as cabbage and nasturtium, but it is difficult to deal with them as pests because their numbers are reinforced from time to time by immigrants from the Continent.

The green-veined white *P. napi*, another widespread and common species, gives no cause for offence, its food-plants being such wild herbs as watercress and cuckoo-flower. Damp fields, marshes and sunny parts of light woodland are among the habitats of this insect, which, like the large and small whites, occurs not only on the mainland but on Lundy and the Isles of Scilly.

At a distance the green-veined white may be taken for a female orange-tip *Anthocharis cardamines*, but the male of this last-named butterfly is quite unmistakable, each of its fore-wings bearing a large patch of orange colour. This delicate and delightful insect, whose food-plants include cuckoo-flower and hedge garlic, adds considerably to the charm of West Country lanes in spring.

One of the earliest butterflies to be seen in the region, the brimstone *Gonepteryx rhamni* is widely distributed. Adults (winged insects) hibernate in ivy or evergreen bushes, emerging in spring when pairing takes place. The eggs are laid on the underside of leaves of alder and purging buckthorns, but the bright sulphur-yellow males and greenish-yellow females are sometimes seen on the wing far from places where these food-plants grow.

Variously described as shy and elusive, delicate and rather insignificant-looking, the wood white *Leptidea sinapis* is locally common in the West Country. Flying in shady woods and woodland margins, it is the only British butterfly that is adapted to spend its whole life under the thick cover of trees. The wood white's larval food-plants are bird's-foot trefoil, tufted vetch and several related species.

The clouded yellow *Colias crocea*, a migrant insect, arrives in varying numbers each year from the Continent. Occasionally the Bath white *Pontia daplidice*, another migrant species, reaches the region.

Some much better-known West Country butterflies are included in the great family the Nymphalidae. The peacock butterfly *Inachis io*, its brownish-red wings bearing 'peacock eyes', is a familiar visitor to flowers in town and country. After hibernating in hollow trees or buildings adult peacock butterflies emerge and pair, the females then laying their eggs on the stinging nettle. Leaves of this common herb are also eaten by larvae of the small tortoiseshell *Aglais urticae*, a pretty butterfly which is seen in parks and gardens on flowers of such plants as Japanese stonecrop and butterfly bush (Buddleja). Small tortoiseshells hibernate as adults and they may be seen fluttering at windows in houses on sunny winter days. Their numbers, like those of the green-veined white and a few other resident butterflies, are increased by immigrants from the Continent.

Unable to maintain themselves in this country, the red admiral *Vanessa atalanta* and the painted lady *V. cardui* depend on immigrants that cross the

* The scientific names are those used in *A field guide to the butterflies of Britain and Europe* (Higgins and Riley).

Channel fairly regularly in spring. Larvae of the red admiral, a beautiful butterfly with its contrasting red, black and white, feed on stinging nettles, while those of the painted lady do so on several types of thistle.

Attractive with its jagged wing shape and unmistakable with a white comma-like mark on the underside of the hind wing, the comma butterfly *Polygonia c-album* is fairly widely distributed and locally common in the region. With woodland as its original home, it is now also seen in lanes and gardens, where its larvae feed on nettle, hop or currant. This species passes the winter in the adult state, hibernating on branches or among dead leaves.

The purple emperor *Apatura iris* was, according to John Burton's survey (1971), in danger of extinction in Somerset. He reported that the species had been re-discovered in one of the old North Mendip localities a few years earlier, but in very small numbers. However, the Biological Record Centre's provisional distribution map for this large and beautiful insect (1975) records no sighting of it in the West Country since 1960. One wonders whether the purple emperor, which flies around the tops of the deciduous trees in old woodland, has eluded

Orange tip butterfly resting.

Small tortoiseshell, whose larvae eat nettles.

observers in recent years, whether it survives at 'secret' sites or whether, as elsewhere, it has disappeared where broad-leaved trees have been replaced by conifers.

The white admiral *Limenitis camilla*, another fine butterfly, is locally distributed in the region, but it is not common. A graceful flier, it is seen on the wing in the rides of broad-leaved woodland. After feeding on honeysuckle the larva spends the winter on a leaf, which it spins together with silk and attaches to a stem. In spring it resumes feeding and development. There have been very few West Country records of the large tortoiseshell *Nymphalis polychloros* since 1960 and one can hold out very little hope for the recovery of the species now that so many of its principal food-plants, elms, have died from disease.

A specimen of the Camberwell beauty *N. antiopa*, a rare vagrant in this country, was seen at Lanhydrock, Cornwall, in 1976, an outstanding year for the large and magnificent butterfly in Britain. Another was sighted in the North Petherton area of Somerset in 1977.

Several fritillaries are common, although often only locally, in the region, the silver-washed fritillary *Argynnis paphia* being, perhaps, the most widely distributed there. Black-spotted and tawny, this large butterfly flies in the rides and open spaces of broad-leaved woods, where its larvae feed on violets. These herbs are also eaten by four other West Country fritillaries, namely the dark green, high brown, pearl-bordered and small pearl-bordered types.

An inhabitant of flowery meadows, moorland and sea-cliffs, the dark green fritillary *Mesoacidalia aglaja* is fairly widespread and has been recorded on Lundy. The high brown fritillary *Fabriciana adippe*, a species of woodland clearings, meadows and sometimes even gardens, is locally distributed, being particularly well represented in south Devon. The pearl-bordered and small pearl-bordered fritillaries, *Clossiana euphrosyne* and *C. selene*, enliven sunny

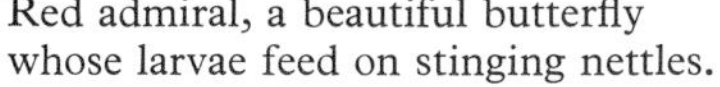

Red admiral, a beautiful butterfly whose larvae feed on stinging nettles.

Heath fritillary, an endangered species that survives in the West Country.

woodland clearings in many parts of the region, the last-named being the more widespread of the two.

As its name suggests, the marsh fritillary *Euphydryas aurinia* prefers flowery meadows and other damp places where its larval food-plant, devil's-bit scabious, may be found. A species that is fairly widespread in the West Country, it is one of the comparatively few British butterflies whose eggs are laid in large clusters. When alarmed its gregarious larvae jerk their heads simultaneously, action which may help to deter predatory birds.

The West Country has most of the remaining British sites of the heath fritillary *Mellicta athalia*, but it is both local and rare, a species that is often considered to be endangered. The heath fritillary haunts woodland clearings and heathy borders, its larvae feeding on common cow-wheat, a widely distributed herb. Unscrupulous collectors and pheasants have been blamed for this butterfly's decline and it is possible that it has suffered from the neglect of coppices, whose regular cutting produced the partially cleared areas which this insect likes.

In the West Country the Duke of Burgundy fritillary *Hamearis lucina*, sole European representative of another family, the Nemeobiidae, flies in a few Somerset woods. Its main larval food-plant is the cowslip, but primrose leaves are eaten too.

A very large family of butterflies whose larvae feed on various grasses, the Satyridae, is represented in the region by eight species, most of them fairly widely distributed. White with blackish markings, as its name suggests, the marbled white *Melanargia galathea* is locally common in grassy places. On hatching the larva of this sedentary insect eats its egg-shell and then goes into hibernation, eating nothing more until the spring, when it feeds on such grasses as Timothy and cock's-foot. Abundant in many districts, the grayling *Hipparchia semele* is seen on cliff-tops, dry heaths and sand-dunes, where it sits, often on bare ground, in the sunshine.

Meadow brown, a butterfly of meadows and grassy places.

Gatekeepers (or hedge browns) mating.

The meadow brown *Maniola jurtina*, an inhabitant of meadows and grassy places, is widespread and common throughout the region, Lundy and the Isles of Scilly included. Scientists who studied West Country meadow browns, among them those of the Isles of Scilly, made some fascinating observations on the distribution of spotting on the underside of the hind-wings. Details of this work and its significance is contained in Professor E. B. Ford's important New Naturalist volumes *Butterflies* and *Moths* (see Bibliography).

The ringlet *Aphantopus hyperantus*, another widespread species, is locally common in the West Country. Favouring lanes, meadows, woodland rides and other damp grassy places, this butterfly (unlike most British species) scatters its eggs as it flies.

Also known as the hedge brown, the gatekeeper *Pyronia tithonus* occurs along hedgerows and grassy woodland rides in most districts. The small heath *Coenonympha pamphilus*, a little butterfly of open grassy places, is ubiquitous. Widespread and common, the speckled wood *Pararge aegeria* prefers the shady parts of woods and lanes. It is the only British butterfly that can hibernate in either of two stages, the larva or the pupa. The wall brown *Lasiommata megera*, a widespread and locally common species that is sometimes called simply the wall butterfly, is often seen basking in sunny places.

The chalk-hill and adonis blues, *Lysandra coridon* and *L. bellargus*, members of the next family to be considered (the Lycaenidae), are confined to calcareous areas. They survive on the eastern fringes of the region, but their numbers have fallen dramatically, largely as the result of the destruction of some habitats by ploughing and the severe modification of others when, after the reduction of the rabbit population by myxomatosis, coarse vegetation grew unchecked.

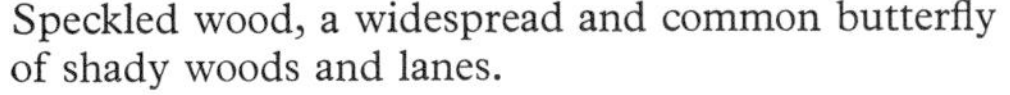

Speckled wood, a widespread and common butterfly of shady woods and lanes.

This butterfly, the large blue, is now protected by law.

The small blue *Cupido minimus* and the brown argus *Aricia agestis* are not restricted to calcareous places, though they certainly prefer them. Nowadays the small blue, whose food-plant is the kidney vetch, is locally distributed along the south Devon coast and in Somerset. The brown argus, a delightful little dark brown butterfly, is locally common in west Cornwall, south Devon and Somerset. Common rock-rose is absent from the greater part of the West Country and larvae of the brown argus feed mainly on their alternative food-plant, common stork's-bill, a herb that favours sandy places near the sea.

Since 1960 the large blue *Maculinea arion*, always a rare species in Britain, has been recorded at a few sites on the north coast of the region, though, as mentioned earlier in connection with the influence of grazing rabbits, it has been considered necessary to give it legal protection. Equally important are the plans to maintain and improve sites of existing large blue colonies and to recover those where the butterfly once bred.

Locally distributed in the region, the silver-studded blue *Plebejus argus* is most likely to be seen in west Cornwall and south Devon (in Somerset it has been classified as in danger of extinction). A characteristic species of dry open heather moors, it also occurs on grassy banks and by the seashore. Rather more widespread, the holly blue *Celastrina argiolus* is locally common in light woodland and large gardens, where the larvae feed on holly, ivy and occasionally such other plants as buckthorn and bramble.

The common blue *Polyommatus icarus*, whose principal food-plants are restharrow and bird's-foot trefoil, flies in meadows and other open spaces. It is widely distributed on the West Country mainland and also occurs on Lundy and the Isles of Scilly. The population of the common blue on the uninhabited island of Tean, Isles of Scilly, was studied some forty years ago by Professor E. B. Ford and his colleague W. H. Dowdeswell, who used this small species in pioneer work on the marking of butterflies (this was done with dots of cellulose paint). Details will be found in the New Naturalist volume *Butterflies*.

Active and alert, the small copper *Lycaena phlaeas* is seen in most parts of the region, where is basks on flowery banks and open ground. Its green larvae feed on broad-leaved dock and sorrel, and hibernate in various stages of development.

The green and purple hairstreaks are both fairly widely distributed in the West Country and common in places. Gorsy woodland borders and rough ground with gorse and broom are typical habitats of the green hairstreak *Callophrys rubi*, whose larvae feed on certain members of the Leguminosae and several other plants. The underside of this butterfly is a beautiful green, a colour closely matching that of the leaves on which it rests. The purple hairstreak *Quercusia quercus* is closely associated with oakwoods, the oak being its principal food-plant.

Very much a local species, the brown hairstreak *Thecla betulae* flies along woodland paths and margins and about thickets, hedges and other places where its larval food-plant, blackthorn, grows. The white-letter hairstreak *Strymonidia w-album* has been recorded from comparatively few West Country sites in recent years, and unfortunately disease has destroyed many of its food-plants, elms.

Grassy banks, rough fields and meadows are typical habitats of the large and small skippers and these widespread butterflies may also be seen flying in woodland rides. The large skipper *Ochlodes venatus* is tawny-yellow, while the small skipper *Thymelicus sylvestris* is better described as brownish-orange. Their larvae feed on certain grasses. Two other skippers, the dingy and the grizzled, are somewhat locally and patchily distributed in the region, where they haunt flowery banks, rough fields and meadows. The dingy skipper *Erynnis tages*, a little dark brown insect, is inconspicuous and moth-like when resting, its wings closed down over its back. In August, after feeding on bird's-foot trefoil, its larva draws leaves together with silk. After sheltering in this 'tent' until April, it becomes a pupa and later the winged insect emerges. The grizzled skipper *Pyrgus malvae*, blackish and white-spotted, sits with the wings erect over its back. Wild strawberry, bramble and a few other species serve as food-plants of the larvae.

The Lulworth skipper *Thymelicus acteon*, whose food-plants are the grasses bushgrass, slender false-brome and couch-grass, has been seen in one or two places in south Devon in recent years. First discovered in this country near Lulworth Cove in 1832, this insect is a true coastal species in England. The Essex skipper *T. lineola* has been recorded from several West Country localities, most of them coastal. Like those of the Lulworth skipper, larvae of the Essex skipper feed on grasses. The silver-spotted skipper *Hesperia comma* was formerly recorded from Somerset limestone areas.

An alder growing by a Devon stream.

Trees and Shrubs

The West Country is not on the whole densely clothed with trees, even Devon being regarded by foresters as no more than fairly well-wooded. There are, however, many places where trees and shrubs form important elements in the vegetation. As the following notes suggest, they also affect other living things in ways that are both numerous and significant.

ALDER *Alnus glutinosa* This inhabitant of streamsides, lakesides, marshes and damp woods is widely distributed. Species associated with it include redpolls and siskins, which enjoy the seeds in autumn and winter, and mites, whose galls appear as reddish bead-like structures on the leaves. Alder roots help to stabilize banks of waterways, and the stems that grow from stumps of coppiced trees make sheltered nesting sites for waterbirds.

ALDER BUCKTHORN *Frangula alnus* This shrub's berries satisfy birds, while its flowers attract insects, including bees. A species of moist commons, the edges of damp woodland and bogs, and limestone scrub, it is a principal food-plant of larvae of the brimstone, a lovely butterfly and a true harbinger of spring. Two other butterflies associated with it are the holly blue, whose larvae eat the flowers, and the green hairstreak, whose larvae are more interested in the contents of the berries.

Alder buckthorn, a principal foodplant of the lovely brimstone butterfly.

Silver birches, comparatively short-lived trees, that yield food for birds and insects.

ASH *Fraxinus excelsior* Though the species is widespread in the region, many of the trees have never been managed for timber production. Some very fine examples of the species have, however, been grown on the Dartington Hall estate in Devon. Large stretches, including Cornwall, are without pure ash-woods, but examples are found on the limestone of the Mendips. One of the best is at Rodney Stoke National Nature Reserve, two miles south-east of Cheddar, where ash grows in association with pedunculate oak, wych elm, whitebeam and field maple. Another interesting West Country ashwood developed in the Axmouth–Lyme Regis Undercliffs National Nature Reserve, Devon, at the site of the great landslip of 1839, in the 'chasm' between the vast slipped block of chalk and greensand and the cliff-top. Ashes produce an open canopy, which allows light to reach the ground and thus permits shrubs and herbs to flourish beneath the trees. At times bullfinches eat large numbers of ash seeds, as do mice and voles.

BARBERRY *Berberis vulgaris* Very locally distributed in the region, this spiny shrub is occasionally seen in hedges. Various insects are attracted to the yellow-flowers.

BEECH *Fagus sylvatica* A widely distributed tree, beech occurs in West Country woods and hedge banks, effective windbreaks which, sadly, in some parts are giving way to wire fences. Beeches are beautiful trees whose leaves change from golden-yellow to dark green and finally to orange-brown. In winter large flocks of chaffinches and bramblings may often be seen feeding on fallen beech mast. Greenfinches and pheasants also enjoy these seeds, as do certain mammals.

BILBERRY *Vaccinium myrtillus* This deciduous shrub is common on West Country heaths and moors and in drier parts of woods on acid soils. The pinkish flowers secrete nectar freely and are naturally attractive to honeybees and bumblebees. Later in the year the purple-black berries are enjoyed by grouse, pheasants and other birds.

BIRCHES *Betula* species Both the silver birch *Betula pendula* and the downy birch *B. pubescens* are widely, if patchily, distributed in the West Country. These trees, with their light, wind-borne seeds, are pioneers that readily colonize many types of ground, high moorland included. Light demanding, birches may in time be shaded out by other species. Even so, they cause clearance problems for conservationists who wish to encourage plants, birds and other creatures that need open conditions. Birches are commonly attacked by a heart-rot fungus whose white, bracket-shaped fruiting bodies appear on trunks and branches. During their comparatively short lives, though, birches yield food in the form of seeds for goldfinches, bullfinches, siskins and other birds. Their leaves are eaten by larvae of several insects, some producing intricate mining patterns as they feed between the outermost layers.

BLACKTHORN *Prunus spinosa* A widespread and common shrub, blackthorn grows in woods and hedges and on waste ground and tops and slopes of cliffs, in

Cotoneaster microphyllus. This plant is growing on limestone on the Devon coast.

places forming dense low scrub. The snowy white flowers, good sources of nectar and pollen to bees, and the buds are eaten by bullfinches. The fruit, the small, very sour sloes, are neglected by many creatures, but hawfinches are able to crack the hard seeds. Larvae of a scarce butterfly, the brown hairstreak, feed on the leaves. (Other members of the genus *Prunus* that grow in scattered West Country localities include wild plum *P. domestica*, wild cherry or gean *P. avium* (birds love its small fruits) and sour cherry *P. cerasus*.)

BOG MYRTLE *Myrica gale* Also called sweet gale, this fragrant deciduous shrub grows in bogs and wet valleys, but it is only locally common in the region.

BRAMBLES *Rubus fruticosus* agg. The West Country flora includes some of the numerous species of bramble or blackberry which have been described and whose serious study is work for specialists. Brambles grow in most parts of the region, single or in dense thickets, in many kinds of habitat, including woods, hedges and waste places. The bushes form nesting sites and places of refuge for wildlife. Bramble flowers attract a large number of insect species, among them bees and butterflies, and the fruits are eaten by birds and also by mammals such as foxes and fallow deer (not to mention man). Greenfinches and bullfinches consume the seeds, usually discarding the pulpy part of the fruit. Brambles are food-plants of the larvae of holly blue, green hairstreak and grizzled skipper butterflies, and deer are among the larger animals that browse on the bushes. Despite their usefulness to other forms of wildlife, brambles are sometimes removed from areas in nature reserves where they show signs of excluding less competitive species.

BROOM *Cytisus scoparius* This yellow-flowered shrub is fairly widespread in the region. It is seen in a variety of habitats, among them open spaces in woods and plantations (until shaded out by growing trees), heathy places and old mining areas, quarries and china-clay workings. The subspecies *maritimus*, with its prostrate stems and densely silky leaves and young twigs, grows on cliffs in west Cornwall and on Lundy. Broom flowers are visited by bees, and larvae of the green hairstreak butterfly feed on the plant.

BUTTERFLY BUSH *Buddleja davidii* This native of China is naturalized in coastal areas, quarries and waste places, where, as its popular name suggests, the dense spikes of fragrant mauve flowers attract numerous butterflies.

COTONEASTERS Introduced as a garden plant, the low evergreen shrub *Cotoneaster microphyllus*, a native of the Himalaya, is naturalized in several parts of the region, where it occurs on spoil heaps and waste ground. *C. simonsii*, a native of India, also grows in the wild in a few places. Bees collect nectar from Cotoneaster flowers and birds eat the colourful fruit.

Dogwood, a species of calcareous soils, photographed at Anstey's Cove, Devon.

CRAB APPLE *Malus sylvestris* Many West Country hedgebanks and copses are enlivened with the beautiful flowers of this wild apple. Bullfinches feed on the small tree's flowers and buds and members of the thrush family eat its fruits.

CURRANTS In the region black currant *Ribes nigrum*, a strong smelling shrub, is a somewhat localized species of hedges and wooded valleys. A good bee plant, its flowers yield both nectar and pollen. Some of the buds are eaten by bullfinches. The condition known as big-bud affects others when they are attacked by mites. The red currant *Ribes rubrum* grows in some West Country woods.

DOGWOOD *Cornus sanguinea* This species of woods and scrub on calcareous soils is locally distributed, the rocky slopes of the Mendips being numbered among its strongholds. An insect-pollinated shrub, it supports a number of insects. Larvae of the holly blue feed on the flowers and those of the green hairstreak on the buds, and a tiny gall midge causes flask-shaped galls that project from the leaves.

DOUGLAS FIR *Pseudotsuga menziesii* This native of western North America has been grown successfully in Eggesford Forest (Devon), Quantock Forest (Somerset) and in several other parts of the West Country. The needles sometimes bear patches of white wool, the hiding-places of the aphid *Adelges cooleyi*.

DUKE OF ARGYLL'S TEA-PLANT *Lycium barbarum* and *L. chinense* These introduced shrubs are naturalized in several places, where their purple flowers and scarlet berries attract attention.

ELDER *Sambucus nigra* Numerous small insects visit the strongly scented flowers of this common species, and others cause mine-patterns on the leaves and galls on the flower-buds. Where other forms of wildlife are concerned, this shrub (or small tree) is, in fact, far from being the worthless weed that many people consider it to be. The purple berries satisfy starlings and other hungry birds, which drop the seeds and thus promote the elder's dispersal in gardens, woods and waste places. Growing on elder one commonly finds the jew's-ear, a fungus that, depending on the weather, is either hard and shrivelled or soft and ear-like. The tree, even on its smallest twigs, may also support a variety of lichens and mosses.

ELMS Various forms of elm have been planted in avenues and used in other ornamental and amenity schemes in the West Country, but those most likely to be seen there are the wych elm *Ulmus glabra* and the English elm *U. procera*, both fairly widespread, and the Cornish elm *U. carpinifolia* var. *cornubiensis*, a common tree in Cornish hedgerows. In the region, as in other parts of the country, many elms have died as the result of Dutch elm disease. Caused by the fungus *Ceratostomella ulmi*, which is spread by the bark beetle *Scolytus scolytus*, the disease, first noted in Holland some three years earlier, reached England about 1927. Several millions of British elms have since died of it, and a

Above
English elms in Devon where, as in other parts of the country, many of these fine trees have died.

Left
Guelder rose, whose shining red berries are eaten by birds.

more aggressive strain appears to have developed in recent years. There seems little doubt that a lot more elms will be lost and many of their replacements will probably be oaks. One can only hope that control measures in force will help to ensure the survival of some elms, for they are not only attractive trees but food-plants of several interesting insects, including white-letter hairstreak and comma butterflies. Bees collect early pollen from the flowers, and at least six species of finch eat the seeds (the bullfinch also feeds on elm buds and flowers).

FIELD MAPLE *Acer campestre* This species is widely distributed in Somerset but somewhat scarce in Cornwall and much of west Devon. Like the sycamore, it attracts the hawfinch and gall-causing mites.

GOOSEBERRY *Ribes uva-crispa* Growing in damp woods and on sheltered hedge-banks, this spiny shrub is fairly widespread in the region. Though inconspicuous, the greenish flowers are attractive to bees for their nectar. Bullfinches eat the buds and several birds take the bristly fruit.

GORSES Despite its dense, spinous nature, the gorse *Ulex europaeus* is often stunted by constant exposure to the wind and in severe winters it may turn brown. Yet there are few districts where the yellow blossom of this common and widespread shrub cannot be found. Bees and bumblebees collect pollen from the flowers. Growing on cliff-tops, moorland, and quarry, mine and china-clay workings, gorse bushes serve as nesting sites for many birds, among them the linnet and the Dartford warbler, and as roosts for finches and other species. A second type of gorse, western gorse *U. gallii*, is widespread and abundant in the region. Unlike *U. europaeus*, which does so in winter and spring, it flowers in late summer and autumn.

GUELDER ROSE *Viburnum opulus* Many kinds of insects visit the white flowers and later birds feed on the shining red berries. Fairly widely distributed in the region, this shrub prefers woods, hedges and scrub where the soil is reasonably damp.

HAWTHORN *Crataegus monogyna* This species is widespread and abundant in the West Country. There are, in fact, times when conservationists and others regard it as an unwanted invader. Often ignored when it is not bearing its strongly scented white blossom, the hawthorn helps to shelter and support a large number of wild creatures. Many kinds of insects are associated with this small tree or shrub. Numerous species visit the flowers, bees sometimes finding them rich in nectar, and many others feed on the leaves, some causing galls, others leaf-mining patterns. The fruits, crimson haws, are eaten by thrushes, hawfinches and other birds and such mammals as grey squirrels and wood mice.

HAZEL *Corylus avellana* Widely distributed in West Country woods and hedges, this is nearly always seen as a much-branched shrub. Formerly cut (coppiced) on a rotational system, to harvest the useful stems, many hazel coppices have long been neglected in the region (as indeed they have in other parts of the country). Cutting encourages the growth of bluebells, primroses and other colourful spring flowers in the coppices. With this in mind, the nature conservation trusts are studying the effects of coppicing and cutting hazels on a few of their reserves on a rotational basis. The Devon Trust has carried out such work at Lady's Wood, South Brent, a small wood which had been coppiced until the 1930s, while the Somerset Trust has undertaken a similar project at Asham Wood. Hazels flower early in the year, when bees visit the male catkins to collect the light yellow pollen. Later the foliage attracts leaf-mining insects, whose larvae feed inside the leaves. The nuts are eaten by nuthatches and such mammals as dormice, wood mice, bank voles and squirrels, each well able to open the hard shells.

HEATHS AND HEATHERS Ling or heather *Calluna vulgaris*, an evergreen shrub, is often a dominant member of the flora of West Country heaths, moors, open woods and industrial wasteland on well-drained acid soils. In some areas (for example, Exmoor) it is subjected to controlled burning ('swaling') to encourage the production of new growth for the benefit of grazing livestock. Ling is also eaten by deer, being particularly important to them in winter, and by the larvae of several moths, one of which, the oak eggar, is a very fine insect. The flowers, generally purple but occasionally white, are popular with bees, bumblebees and a number of other insects. Heather seeds are minute, but there are times when bullfinches eat large quantities of them. Grouse eat heather shoots, flowers and seed-heads.

Cross-leaved heath or bog heather *Erica tetralix* is another widespread species. A rose-pink-flowered shrub, it grows mainly in bogs and on wet heaths and moors. The flowers attract insect visitors, but the plant itself is not always as popular with grazing animals as ling. Bell heather *E. cinerea*, an evergreen shrub with crimson-purple flowers, is widely distributed on dry heaths and moors and occasionally occurs in dry woods. Dorset heath *E. ciliaris*, with deep pink flowers, is a very local species of moors in west Cornwall and south Devon, while Cornish heath *E. vagans*, its flowers of various shades of lilac, occurs in many parts of the Lizard peninsula.

HOLLY *Ilex aquifolium* Many birds eat the berries and one of them, the hawfinch, leaves split stones beneath the trees. The flowers of holly, a fairly common species of West Country woods and hedges, secrete abundant nectar and are much visited by bees. The leaves are eaten by larvae of a mining fly and those of the holly blue butterfly, and deer find them quite palatable, especially in winter, when they also gnaw the bark.

HORNBEAM *Carpinus betulus* An uncommon tree in the West Country, this may on occasion be confused with the beech, though the two species are quite distinct. Hawfinches and greenfinches are known to eat its fruits.

HORSE CHESTNUT *Aesculus hippocastanum* This stately tree has been used for decorative effect in West Country parks, avenues and roadside situations. Its flowers, whose 'candles' or spikes make it a beautiful sight, are well worked by bees collecting pollen and nectar. The nuts are usually left to small boys for use in games of conkers!

KARO *Pittosporum crassifolium* A dark red-flowered native of New Zealand, this erect fast-growing shrub is naturalized in Scilly, where it was planted as a bulbfield windbreak. The seeds are apparently distributed by birds, young plants being found in many places, even on uninhabited islands.

LARCHES The Forestry Commission and other landowners have planted in West Country woods three types of larch, deciduous conifers which, casting a light shade, allow ferns, grasses and certain other plants to grow beneath them. The European larch *Larix decidua* has emerald green needles that turn golden in autumn and straw-coloured or ashen-grey twigs. A faster growing species, the Japanese larch *L. kaempferi* is known by its bluish-green foliage and russet twigs. The offspring of the European and Japanese larches, the Dunkeld hybrid larch *L. x eurolepis*, is another fast-growing tree, examples of which may be seen on the National Trust's Killerton property in Devon and on the Pencarrow estate near Bodmin. A number of insects and fungi are associated with larches and squirrels and crossbills enjoy the seeds.

LAWSON CYPRESS *Chamaecyparis lawsoniana* This North American conifer is planted as an ornamental tree and also as a timber producer. Some fine specimens grow in the West Country.

LIMES Lime trees, many of them planted in parks, gardens and churchyards, may be seen in scattered localities in the region. Very often the species involved is the common lime *Tilia x vulgaris*, a hybrid of the small-leaved and large-leaved limes. Nowadays limes are rarely planted for timber, but they are valued as amenity trees. Honey bees and bumblebees collect nectar from the fragrant flowers, but in a concentrated form this is mildly toxic and foraging bees, especially bumblebees, may become drowsy and more likely to be preyed on by shrikes and certain other birds. In summer aphids feeding on lime leaves secrete sweet sticky honeydew, which is often discoloured by sooty moulds. The leaves themselves commonly bear galls caused by mites and gall-midges.

NEEDLE FURZE (or petty whin) *Genista anglica* A spiny and yellow-flowered species of heaths and moors, this small shrub is a food-plant of the green hairstreak butterfly.

OAKS The pedunculate oak *Quercus robur*, with stalked flowers and acorns and stalkless leaves, the sessile oak *Q. petraea*, with unstalked flowers and acorns and stalked leaves, and hybrids between them are the region's leading trees. Many West Country oaks grow on the steep sides of river valleys. Some of them are well-grown individuals, but others, short-boled and branchy, form coppices which, cut over at regular intervals, yielded firewood, bark for tanning and other products. There are in the West Country a few oakwoods which may truly be called famous. Wistman's Wood, a Forest Nature Reserve on the side of the West Dart valley above Two Bridges, is one such place. Dwarf, thick-trunked pedunculate oaks have long survived in this high exposed wood, which has doubled in area since 1905. Growing on trunks and branches are mosses, liverworts, lichens, ferns and several species of flowering

Pedunculate oaks in Wistman's Wood, Dartmoor.

plants, some of them also appearing on the granite boulders between which the trees are rooted.

Many different birds find shelter and nesting sites in West Country oaks, and some, such as jays, rooks and woodpigeons, feed on acorns. Squirrels and certain other mammals also enjoy these seeds and, like some of the birds concerned, may bury acorns, leaving a number to germinate and develop into seedling oaks. Numerous species of insects feed upon oak. Larvae of the purple hairstreak, a species that is widespread and fairly common in the West Country, eat the leaves and the butterflies themselves enjoy flying high above the treetops. Some insect larvae create mine patterns on the leaves as they feed inside them, and many types of gall-wasp cause galls to appear on leaves, stems, flowers and roots of oaks. Pheasants pick spangle-galls from fallen oak leaves and tits attack the hard round marble galls to get at the gall-wasp larvae within.

Several other types of oak are found in the West Country. In the Exeter district there are some 200-year-old specimens of the Turkey oak *Q. cerris*. Introduced to Britain from Asia Minor in 1735, this species with 'mossy' acorn cups also occurs on Lundy and elsewhere in the region. The holm oak *Q. ilex*, an evergreen tree introduced from southern Europe about 1500, resists seawinds and has been planted for ornament.

Left
Foliage of wild service tree, Devon.

Below
Privet, showing the white flowers which are followed by shining black berries.

PERIWINKLES The lesser and greater periwinkles, *Vinca minor* and *V. major*, grow on banks and in woods in many districts. Long-tongued bees, bee-flies and other insects visit the blue-purple flowers.

PINES The Scots pine *Pinus sylvestris* has been planted in many parts of the West Country and is naturalized in several of them. Our only native coniferous or softwood tree of value for timber production, it has done quite well on the sands and gravels of Haldon Hill in south Devon, on poor moorland pastures in north Devon, and on other infertile soils elsewhere in the region. The tree produces a fairly dense shade throughout the year and its fallen needles sometimes take a long time to decay. Not surprisingly, therefore, comparatively few smaller plants grow beneath it. A number of insects are associated with the species and its seeds are eaten by squirrels and various finches.

The Corsican pine *P. nigra* var. *maritima*, a native of south-west Europe, is grown in several parts of the region as a general-purpose softwood. A native of western North America, the lodgepole pine *P. contorta* var. *latifolia* is capable of growing in very exposed places. The Forestry Commission has planted it in several of its plantations and since the 1960s it has been grown as a windbreak on the Isles of Scilly.

The Californian Monterey pine *P. radiata* is abundant in the region, especially near the coast. Wind-resisting and capable of rapid growth, it was used to form shelterbelts on the Isles of Scilly. It has grown well on the Dartington Hall estate in Devon, and has produced natural seedlings near Marazion in Cornwall. The impressive maritime pine *P. pinaster*, a native of the Mediterranean area, has been planted in a number of West Country localities and has spread by means of its large wind-borne seeds on to certain heaths.

POPLARS Several poplars, a number of them introduced and planted species, are seen in the West Country, where the resistance of some varieties to sea winds has made them excellent trees for amenity use and shelter. The aspen *Populus tremula*, the grey poplar *P. canescens*, the white poplar *P. alba* and forms of the black poplar *P. nigra* agg. are among those growing in woods, parks, gardens and other situations. There are trial plots of many different varieties of poplar, some of them extra-fast growing, in the valley bottom at the Forestry Commission's King's Cliff Wood, near North Petherton, on the Quantocks. Among the many insects associated with poplars are large tortoiseshell and purple emperor butterflies and gall-causing aphids.

PRIVET *Ligustrum vulgare* Like snowberry, privet forms thickets which provide nesting sites for birds and shelter for certain mammals. Insects pollinate the strongly scented white flowers of this fairly widespread shrub and birds devour the shining black berries, bullfinches being very found of the seeds.

RASPBERRY *Rubus idaeus* As a wild plant, this prickly shrub is scarce in Cornwall, but less so in other parts of the West Country mainland. Various insects visit its white flowers, a source of nectar and pollen to bees, and larvae of the grizzled skipper butterfly feed on the leaves. The fruit are eaten by birds.

RHODODENDRON *Rhododendron ponticum* Well known for its large, brown-spotted purple flowers, this introduced evergreen has become well established on the West Country mainland and on Tresco and Lundy. It has, in fact, become so dominant in certain woods that foresters and conservationists often go to considerable trouble in attempting to eradicate it. Spreading by means of its small seeds, the species has colonized roadsides, waste ground and other open spaces. Birds and mammals shelter in the thickets it forms and insects visit the flowers. Bumblebees can reach the nectar, but honeybees can only do so when it is secreted copiously.

ROWAN *Sorbus aucuparia* Also called mountain ash, this common small tree of woods and moorlands bears clusters of white flowers. The bright red berries are enjoyed by blackbirds and thrushes and opened by bullfinches and crossbills which feed on the seeds. The rowan's close relative, the wild service tree *S. torminalis*, is very locally distributed in the region, but it is well worth looking for.

SEA BUCKTHORN *Hippophaë rhamnoides* This silvery-leaved shrub occurs on dunes north of Hayle in Cornwall and at several other places on West Country coasts. The small greenish flowers are wind-pollinated, but some insects visit them. Birds eat the orange-coloured fruit.

SILVER FIRS Many West Country woods, particularly those in Cornwall and north-west Devon, include the common silver fir *Abies alba*. Introduced to Britain from Europe early in the seventeenth century, it is attacked by a minute aphid and is very rarely planted nowadays. The grand fir *A. grandis* and the noble fir *A. procera*, natives of western North America, were introduced in the 1830s. There are some large specimens of the grand fir at Endsleigh, Devon, and Mells Park, Somerset.

SNOWBERRY *Symphoricarpos rivularis* Introduced from North America and planted in hedges and woods, this species spreads by suckers. The common name refers to the globose white berries. These follow the pinkish-white flowers which, despite their smallness, are rich in nectar and very attractive to bees, bumblebees and wasps.

SPINDLE-TREE *Euonymus europaeus* A shrub that prefers calcareous soils, the spindle-tree grows in hedgerows and woodland edges in many parts of the region. Small insects visit its greenish flowers, which are sometimes eaten by larvae of the holly blue butterfly. Unfortunately the spindle-tree is the winter host of the bean or black aphis, a common and widespread pest of beans and many other plants, both cultivated and wild.

SPRUCES The Norway spruce *Picea abies*, the familiar Christmas tree, has been planted in several parts of the region. Its green foliage contrasts with the blue-green needles of the Sitka spruce *P. sitchensis*, a species that also thrives in many West Country situations, including exposed parts of Bodmin Moor and Dartmoor. Plantations of spruce (and indeed of other conifers too) have some-

Tree mallow, a handsome rose-purple-flowered plant, photographed at Berry Head, Devon.

time been regarded as 'dark alien masses' but one should not lose sight of the fact that, while producing timber, they provide shelter for birds and other forms of wildlife in places where many trees would find difficulty in establishing themselves.

SPURGE LAUREL *Daphne laureola* As a West Country plant, this evergreen shrub is mainly confined to Somerset and east Devon. It grows in woods and copses where its green flowers attract bees, butterflies and moths early in the year.

SWEET CHESTNUT *Castanea sativa* This tree has been planted in many of the region's parks and woods. People are not the only mammals that eat the nuts, for they are enjoyed by deer and squirrels too.

SYCAMORE *Acer pseudoplatanus* Common in many parts of the West Country, Lundy and Scilly included, this great maple produces wind-borne seeds that germinate in all sorts of places. As a result gardeners spend time pulling up the seedlings and conservationists are sometimes forced to clear saplings from nature reserves to prevent the ousting of smaller and less aggressive plants. But, despite all this, the sycamore plays its part in the lives of several other species. Its fruits are eaten by that attractive bird the shy and elusive hawfinch and bees collect nectar from the hanging bunches of greenish yellow flowers. Mites cause red pimple-galls and patches of swollen hairs to develop on the leaves, which often bear black 'tar spots' produced by the fungus *Rhytisma acerinum.*

TAMARISK *Tamarix anglica, T. gallica* These introduced shrubs have become established at points on the West Country mainland coasts and on Scilly, where they have been planted as bulbfield windbreaks. Bees collect nectar from the small pink or white flowers.

TREE LUPIN *Lupinus arboreus* This native of California is naturalized on Scilly and parts of the mainland, occurring on dunes, sandy ground and china-clay waste. Many insects visit the large spikes of pale yellow or white flowers.

TREE MALLOW *Lavatera arborea* Handsome with its large pale rose-purple flowers, this tall erect plant is cultivated in gardens. As a wild species, it grows on cliff-slopes and waste ground near the sea on the West Country mainland, Lundy and Scilly. Flowering occurs in the second year, during which the plant completes its life-cycle.

TUTSAN *Hypericum androsaemum* Widely distributed in the region, this yellow-flowered half-evergreen shrub grows in damp woods, hedges and lanes.

WAYFARING TREE *Viburnum lantana* A shrub with cream-white flowers and fruits that eventually become black, this species is seen on the Mendips and in other places with calcareous soils.

WESTERN HEMLOCK *Tsuga heterophylla* Introduced to Britain from western North America in 1851, this tree has been planted in several West Country woods. There are some large specimens in Devon.

WESTERN RED CEDAR *Thuja plicata* This was discovered in 1853 by William Lobb, a Cornishman who was employed by John Veitch, the Exeter nurseryman, to collect seed of the rare and remarkable conifers that had been reported in Oregon and British Columbia. It has done well in the West Country, there being some particularly fine specimens in Devon.

WILD ROSES *Rosa* species Many insects visit the flowers and gall-wasps cause 'robin's pincushions', smooth and spiny 'peas' and other galls on these shrubs.

Common sallow, a honeybee visiting a female catkin, Devon.

A fine crack willow, Devon.

The fruits ('hips') provide food for greenfinches, hawfinches and other birds and also for such small mammals as bank voles and wood mice. A white-flowered species, the field rose *R. arvensis* is widespread in the West Country, as is the pink or white-flowered dog rose *R. canina* agg. The burnet rose *R. pimpinellifolia*, with cream-white (rarely pink) flowers, grows as a low erect shrub, mainly in coastal districts of the region. The downy rose *R. villosa* agg., with flowers that are usually deep pink, and the sweet-briar *R. rubiginosa* agg., whose leaflets are provided with sweet-scented glands, are locally distributed here.

WILLOWS, including osiers and sallows Several members of the genus *Salix*, the trees and shrubs variously known as willows, osiers and sallows, grow in the West Country, where, on Sedgemoor, osiers are still raised for the supple pliant rods used in basketry. The common sallow *S. cinerea* and the goat or pussy willow *S. caprea* are widely distributed species of damp woods and moorland valleys, fieldsides and pondsides. They are a nuisance in plantations where foresters treat them as weeds, and on nature reserves where, given the chance, these invaders quickly transform open areas. A dwarf species, the creeping willow *S. repens*, is widespread on damp moors and heaths. The common osier *S. viminalis* and the eared sallow *S. aurita* are widely distributed, and at least four other species, the white, crack, almond and purple willows, *S. alba*, *S. fragilis*, *S. triandra* and *S. purpurea* respectively, are found in the region.

Honeybees and bumblebees visit catkins of the various *Salix* species, important sources of early pollen and nectar, and certain types of sawfly deposit their eggs in the tissues of the leaves, causing bean-galls to form. The larvae of two very scarce butterflies, the large tortoiseshell and the purple emperor, and those of a commoner and more widespread species, the purple hairstreak, feed on the leaves of some *Salix* species. Redpolls and bullfinches eat sallow buds and flowers in spring.

YEW *Taxus baccata* The dark green foliage of this native tree contributes considerably to the beauty of Cheddar Gorge and other places on the limestone of the Mendips. Elsewhere in the region yews are largely confined to churchyards, where they were planted, often for shelter, sometimes hundreds of years ago. Specimens of exceptional girth have been recorded at Dartington and Mamhead in Devon. Yews cast such a dense shade that few plants grow beneath them. They provide nesting sites for several birds, goldcrests suspending their nests beneath the ends of the branches. Thrushes and other birds enjoy the fruits and greenfinches take the seeds. In winter hawfinches feed on the terminal shoots and deer browse on the foliage. A midge that causes artichoke-galls is one of the few insects associated with yew.

Some other plants

In addition to trees and shrubs, most of which have already been mentioned, the West Country flora includes numerous smaller plants. There are so many that one cannot possibly mention more than a few of them here. In any case, such types as algae, fungi, lichens, mosses and liverworts are outside the scope of this book, and readers who wish to study them should consult specialized publications. Those who wish to interest themselves more seriously in the flowering plants and ferns should refer to county floras or, better still, make use of the *Atlas of the British Flora* (see Bibliography) to prepare lists for the districts or counties with which they are concerned. Then, by attempting to fill in gaps, they may eventually add to our knowledge of plant distribution.

Some readers may be content simply to enjoy the plants, the colours and scents of their flowers, the shapes and textures of their foliage. There is absolutely nothing wrong with this approach. Indeed, the future of this part of our great natural heritage will become increasingly secure as more and more people appreciate its interest and variety.

THE COAST

A good place to begin is at the coast, where land plants flower in profusion and where specialized plants thrive, sometimes in association with more widely distributed species, in habitats such as salt-marshes and sand-dunes. This interesting state of affairs is revealed in a particularly colourful and enjoyable way to those who visit the West Country in May or June.

Everyone has his own favourite places for wild flowers. One of mine is reached by the footpath that runs along the cliffs below the Lizard lighthouse. Here, on slopes above the sea, are bluebells,* whose sweetly scented flowers also enliven so many hedgebanks and woods, red campions and yellow-green-flowered alexanders, an introduced species that was formerly cultivated as a celery-flavoured pot-herb. The plant bearing white bluebell-like flowers is the triquetrous garlic whose name explains why the foliage smells so strongly when crushed. A native of the western Mediterranean region, it is naturalized in places near the sea in Scilly, west Cornwall and several other parts of the region.

Primroses and pinkish-purple-flowered foxgloves also occur on cliff-tops and slopes. The spring squill, with pale blue flowers, and the autumnal squill, its flowers purplish, grow in dry grassy places. Thrift, with its cushions of fine green leaves and masses of rose-pink flowers, does well on rocks, even on tiny ledges and in crevices on vertical cliffs, and on cliff-top walls and banks. At the Lizard, it is associated with English stonecrop, a fleshy-leaved perennial whose white petals are pinkish on the back, and sheep's-bit, its heads of small flowers a beautiful shade of blue.

Wild carrot, common scurvy-grass and sea campion, white-flowered species, grow on cliff-tops and sometimes on steep rocky cliffs and slopes too. The Hottentot fig, a native of South Africa with fleshy leaves and showy magenta or pale yellow flowers, is naturalized on certain West Country cliffs. Some conservationists have pointed out that it smothers and displaces smaller plants. This is, of course, also true of bracken and such shrubs as blackthorn, gorse and ling, each attractive in its own way and each capable of becoming dominant, not only on cliff-tops but in other habitats.

Species of lower cliffs and rocks are not always easily accessible and readers

* The scientific names of plants are listed at the end of the chapter.

Centaury, a pink-flowered annual whose habitats include dunes and dry pastures.

should never forget to exercise great care when looking for them. Rock samphire is well adapted to such situations, its long root anchoring it in crevices, its fleshy leaves retaining moisture. Insects are attracted to its umbrella-shaped heads of nectar-rich yellowish-green flowers. Golden samphire, another succulent plant, makes an even more delightful sight, its flowers composed of golden yellow ray-florets and orange-yellow disk-florets. Rock sea lavender, a close relative of thrift, bears violet-blue flowers and looks far too slender for an inhabitant of spray-washed cliffs and rocks.

Biting stonecrop, with fleshy leaves and bright yellow flowers, a species of sandy places, walls and rocks.

This last-named species grows with such other maritime plants as cliff sea-spurrey, rock samphire and Portland spurge at Beer Head on the south Devon coast. The cliffs here are of chalk and the grassland above them includes such plants as common rockrose, with its bright yellow flowers, and salad burnet. At Berry Head, a point on the south Devon coast where the cliffs are of limestone, there are maritime plants and a limestone flora which includes white rockrose, a very local species with small silvery leaves and, as its name suggests, white flowers.

Sand-dunes, like the habitats already mentioned, are exposed to wind and in the West Country, as elsewhere, they are built up and stabilized by specialized plants. Sand couch-grass is an early pioneer in dune formation. Marram grass, a much more conspicuous plant, is another. Producing a long and complex root system, it throws up new shoots from creeping underground stems when buried by drifting sand. Younger dunes are the habitat of several other interesting species, among them sea bindweed, with trailing stems and pink trumpet-shaped flowers, and sea holly, a plant with spiny silvery leaves and heads of bright blue flowers. These two plants are favourites of bees and other insects, while ragwort, one of many inland species occurring on dunes, attracts the cinnabar, a moth whose purplish black and orange yellow-banded larvae feed on the leaves.

Fixed dunes are colonized by many plants, some with colourful flowers.

Grasses and shrubs may be present and where the sand is rich in shells one may see such lime-loving species as pink-flowered restharrow and pyramidal orchid with spikes of rosy-purple flowers. Rabbits dislike centaury, biting stonecrop, gladdon and certain other plants of fixed dunes, which thrive where more palatable species are kept in check. Different plants grow in dune-slacks. Some of these hollows between dune ridges at Penhale Sands near Perranporth are quite wet and common marsh plants thrive there. Other slacks, some wet, others with moisture just below the surface, have developed at Braunton Burrows National Nature Reserve and Berrow sand-dunes.

Both maritime plants and more generally distributed species grow on shingle, a highly specialized habitat which is particularly well represented at Loe Bar (Cornwall) and Slapton (Devon). Anchored by a stout tap-root, yellow horned poppy produces large yellow flowers and long curved seed-pods (the 'horns'). Sea campion, with its dainty white flowers, forms low mats over shingle, also

Gladdon, whose bright orange or scarlet seeds are more conspicuous than its violet-blue or whitish flowers.

being found on cliffs and sometimes on sand-dunes too. Sea sandwort has fleshy leaves and small cream-coloured flowers, and survives when covered by shingle or sand by throwing up new shoots. Other plants of West Country shingle include the maritime variety of curled dock, a perennial with a thick fleshy rootstock, wild carrot, sea holly and sea kale, a large cabbage-like plant.

The plants of salt-marshes, habitats developed on the mud and sand of many West Country estuaries, are affected by the tides and are subject to submergence by sea-water. A colonizer of mud, glasswort or marsh samphire, a highly succulent species with erect segmented stems, acts as a pioneer in salt-marsh development. In the higher parts of areas where glasswort has become established one sees such plants as common salt-marsh-grass, vigorous and spreading by long runners, and sea aster, a species reminding one of its close relatives, the cultivated michaelmas daisies. These plants trap silt and debris, raising the level of the soil and creating that part of the salt-marsh known as the middle marsh. (In places where conditions are unsuitable for glasswort, Townsend's cord-grass, known also as rice grass, may become completely dominant, excluding other species, and quickly raise the level of the mud-flats.)

Of the species growing on the middle marsh, the most colourful are thrift, already mentioned, and common sea lavender, its beautiful blue-purple flowers attracting bees and other insects. Sea plantain, sea spurrey, common salt-marsh-grass and sea arrow-grass may also be present, as may sea purslane, a shrubby plant with silvery leaves and small yellow flowers. These species also help to build up the general level of the salt-marsh. Some of them may be seen growing in the upper marsh with pink-flowered sea milkwort, mud rush, red or creeping fescue (a widespread and abundant grass) and others.

FRESHWATER HABITATS

The plants of ponds, rivers and similar habitats are not always allowed to grow undisturbed for any length of time, for at intervals ponds are cleaned out and rivers dredged. Even so, one is not usually far from a stretch of fresh water where at least a few aquatic plants may be seen. Widely distributed in the region, the common duckweed, a tiny green circular frond with a single root, floats on stagnant water, often forming a green carpet. On Sedgemoor three other species of duckweed occur, as does Britain's smallest flowering plant, the rootless *Wolffia arrhiza*, a floating pinhead of green. One may also find there the tiny free-floating *Azolla filiculoides*, a bluish-green North American fern that turns red in autumn.

Another North American species, the dark green Canadian pondweed, grows submerged in a number of West Country waters. More conspicuous, with spikes of greenish flowers and both floating and submerged leaves, are bog pondweed, whose name reminds us that its habitats include bog-pools, and broad-leaved pondweed. Even more striking to the eye are plants that project well above the water and sometimes grow on mud beside it. Water plantain is one, its tall branched stems bearing small pale lilac flowers that open in the early afternoon and wither a few hours later. Another is water horsetail, one of several living representatives of plants that were very common and important in the Coal Measure period, when some grew to tree size.

Alders, willows and sallows, trees and shrubs referred to in the previous chapter, often grow at the waterside. Our tallest native grass, the common reed, may be found there, its roots and rhizomes forming a network in the soil. Great reedmace colonizes such places, seeds released from its large brown cylindrical 'pokers' readily germinating in the mud. Bur-reed, its unisexual flowers in separate heads, and reed canary-grass, robust and deep rooting, also occur.

The waterside is often enlivened by such tall and showy species as great hairy willow-herb, whose other name of codlins and cream suits a plant with

Pale butterwort, an insectivorous herb of bogs and wet heaths.

Marsh violet, a perennial herb whose habits are spongy bogs and swampy places in woods.

Heath spotted orchid, a plant of moist acid peaty soils.

flowers of deep purplish-rose. Purple loosestrife and yellow loosestrife, members of different plant families, sport spikes of attractive flowers whose colours are suggested by their names. Marsh woundwort bears spikes of dull purple flowers, while water figwort has brownish-purple flowers, favourites of wasps towards the end of summer. The naturalized Himalayan balsam, named after its native region, produces large purplish-pink flowers, which are visited by bees and butterflies. Well able to spread very quickly, its seeds being scattered explosively, it may become dominant, forcing out many smaller plants.

Despite the competition of larger species, comparatively short plants do survive in many waterside situations. The strongly scented water mint attracts bees, butterflies and other insects to its rounded heads of lilac flowers. Unlike mint, its close relative, gipsy-wort, an erect plant with purple-dotted white flowers, is without scent. The pinkish flowers of butterbur appear before the plant's very large leaves, which often shade out other species. Monkey-flower, a native of western North America, is naturalized at the waterside, where its red-spotted yellow flowers are pollinated by bees.

A few of the plants just mentioned also grow on the mineral soils of marshes and on the organic (peaty) soils of those marshes known as fens. Large areas of these wetland habitats, which are very similar in their vegetation, have been considerably modified by drainage, cultivation, mowing and grazing, the use of fertilizers and herbicides, and the removal of peat deposits. Nowadays, as a result, marsh plants are often confined to such places as ditches, patches of low-lying land in river valleys and poorly drained parts of fields.

Certain sedges and rushes are important marsh plants, but they lack the beauty of the yellow flag, the yellow-flowered wild iris with sword-like leaves. Equally colourful is the marsh marigold or kingcup whose bright golden-

Wild daffodils in Dunsford Wood, a nature reserve of the Devon Trust for Nature Conservation.

yellow flowers, botanically 'primitive', are visited by many kinds of insects for nectar and pollen. Marsh ragwort is another yellow-flowered species, as is marsh fleabane. Meadowsweet, whose cream-white flowers attract insects, often has on its leaves irregular 'beads' and pustules caused by gall midges.

Water forget-me-nots, their flowers sky-blue, common marsh orchid, with tall spikes of bright pinkish-purple flowers, and the creeping pennywort, its leaves rounded, its tiny flowers pinkish, are just a few more plants of marshes, fertile habitats where many mosses also thrive.

Bog-mosses, species of *Sphagnum*, are often abundant on the wet acid peat of bogs. This type of habitat has often been seriously modified and even destroyed in parts of the West Country, but some important examples remain. There are great areas of blanket bog, where peat forms a more or less blanket-like layer, on the northern and southern plateaux of Dartmoor. Valley bogs occur on Dartmoor and in several other districts, while the raised bog, a habitat that rises above the immediate surroundings, is a feature of parts of the Somerset Levels.

Certain members of the sedge family form significant elements in the flora of West Country bogs. When in fruit, common cotton-grass and its close relative, the less widely distributed hare's-tail, bear conspicuous white cottony heads. Then there are deer-grass, densely tufted and slender-stemmed, white beak-sedge, whose whitish spikelets become reddish-brown, and others. Bog myrtle, bilberry and cross-leaved heath, shrubs mentioned in the previous chapter, add to the variety of bog vegetation.

Other bog plants are of considerable interest and some introduce beauty and colour. Tormentil, a slender herb, has yellow flowers and bog asphodel, whose remarkable seeds are long-tailed, has short spikes of fragrant yellow flowers. Bog pimpernel, a tiny plant, creeps over wet mosses, its pale pink bell-like flowers opening on sunny days. Sundews entrap small insects, sources of essential nitrogen, on the sticky hairs of their leaves and secrete juices which digest them. Butterworts, whose main representative in the West Country is the pale butterwort, also use their sticky leaves to trap and digest midges and other tiny insects. Marsh violet bears lilac flowers whose veins are darker.

HEATHS AND MOORS

Bog, heath and moor are interconnected in the sense that drainage or drying out of bog may result in the replacement of bog plants by species more generally associated with heath and moor (also, of course, bog may develop in waterlogged parts of heath and moor). Perhaps the commonest of heath and moor plants is ling or heather, which, like such other heathland and moorland shrubs as bilberry, gorse and various types of heath and heather, is the subject of notes in the previous chapter.

When they grow unchecked, these shrubs exclude many other plants, though lichens and mosses often survive under and among them. Wavy hair-grass, a beautiful plant, the fine-leaved bristle bent-grass and fescue grasses are abundant in places. Heath milkwort, whose flowers may be blue, pink or white, tormentil and heath bedstraw, with its small pure white flowers, are among the herbs.

Bracken, the tall and vigorous fern that shades out so many plants, has invaded large areas of West Country heath and moor. This has resulted, at least in places, from uncontrolled and too frequent moor burning, which severely weakens or kills ling and other plants and encourages the spread of bracken, whose deeply buried rhizomes usually escape undamaged. Gorse often manages to survive these fires, new growth being produced from its burnt stumps and new seedlings from its widely scattered heat-resistant seeds. New growth of ling and grass can be encouraged for the benefit of grazing livestock by carrying out controlled burning in winter or early spring (before the start of the growing season) at intervals of several years.

GRASSLAND

Grass-moors, types of uncultivated acid-grassland, are found on Bodmin Moor, Exmoor and Dartmoor and in other West Country districts. As the name suggests, the important plants are grasses. Purple moor-grass, a very variable species whose young leaves are grazed by cattle and sheep, is often dominant on the wet or damp peaty soils, where it may exclude all other flowering plants. Cotton-grass, deer-grass and rushes flourish where the peat is waterlogged. Where it is well-drained, the dominant plant is usually mat-grass, whose tough wiry foliage only interests grazing animals when it is young. The heath spotted orchid, with spikes of pale pink flowers, their lips with reddish markings, may make an appearance and so may one or two other colourful herbs. Changing conditions may encourage colonization by bracken and shrubs.

Much richer in plant species than grass-moor and other types of acid grassland, calcareous grassland, often fragmentary, occurs in the region on limestone on the Mendips and at Torquay, Berry Head and Plymouth and on chalk along the Branscombe–Beer section of the south Devon coast. Several rarities grow in these places, but much interest and colour is added by commoner plants. There are rock roses, small scabious, with heads of pale purplish-blue flowers, and fragrant wild thyme, its masses of purplish flowers attracting numerous insects. One also finds salad burnet, cowslip, stemless thistle, from whose rosette of prickly leaves rise purplish-red heads of flowers, and many more.

There is in the West Country a lot of cultivated grassland, much of it 'permanent', containing not only the grasses, clovers and other plants that make really productive pasture but species that, from the farmer's point of view, are better regarded as weeds. Docks and thistles are obvious members of this last-named group, as is ragwort, a poisonous plant which animals may be tempted to eat during severe drought. Creeping, meadow and bulbous buttercups, common and widely distributed species, are harmless when dried in hay, but they may prove poisonous to cattle when fresh.

As one might suspect from its name, crow garlic is unwelcome in pastures because of the flavour it imparts to milk. Even yarrow, attractive with finely cut leaves and white or pink flower-heads, may be eaten too freely by cattle, resulting in milk and butter acquiring a bitter aromatic taste. Like yarrow, ribwort plantain, with its lance-shaped leaves and spikes of wind-pollinated flowers, can become dominant in places.

Of course, the vegetation of a pasture depends a lot on the type of soil and the extent to which is is managed (or neglected!). For example, sheep's sorrel,

amsons, a bulbous herb smelling of onion or garlic, rows in damp woods and shady places.

Hard fern growing in Stoke Wood, Exeter.

Hart's-tongue, a fern of woods and shaded banks.

a slender reddish plant whose oxalic acid content may cause poisoning in livestock, does not thrive on pasture that is treated for soil acidity. Again, knapweed, a hard-stemmed perennial with globe-shaped heads of red-purple flowers, is not likely to be abundant in pasture where phosphate deficiency is corrected.

WOODLANDS AND PLANTATIONS

The vegetation of woods and plantations is affected not only by soil type and management but by such other factors as age, height and species of their constituent trees and shrubs. West Country oakwoods and woods of mixed deciduous trees are often rich in plant species. Hazel, sallow and other shrubs may be present, as may ivy and honeysuckle, climbers whose flowers attract insects and whose berries are eaten by birds. Some of the most attractive herbs flower before the trees and shrubs develop their leaves and cut off light from the woodland floor. Dog's mercury with spikes of inconspicuous greenish flowers, carpets the ground in early spring. Primroses, also with bright green leaves, bear sweet-scented flowers of cream-yellow and wild daffodils appear in damp woods.

The bluebell, whose sweet-scented flowers always seem so very blue under Cornish skies in May, makes food while light is plentiful and stores it in its bulb. Wood anemone, its flowers whitish or pinkish, and lesser celandine, with glossy leaves and bright yellow star-like flowers, also appear in the woods.

'endulous sedge, a perennial that grows up to 5 ft high, is easily spotted because of its long pendulous spikelets.

Cuckoo pint is conspicuous in spring (as illustrated) and also when the red berries appear.

Greater stitchwort, a common perennial of woods and hedgerows.

Blue-flowered ground ivy creeps over the woodland floor, and in moist shady places moschatel, small and weak, reveals how it gained the name of town-hall-clock, its flowers being in clusters of five, one terminal, the others facing outwards in four directions. The early purple orchid, curiously also called blue butcher, produces its spike of purplish-crimson flowers and ramsons, a broad-leaved garlic, its loose head of white ones.

As the weeks pass, other herbs come into flower. Wood avens, also called herb Bennet, bears bright yellow flowers, forerunners of fruits whose distribution by people and animals is promoted by hooked prickles that catch on to clothing, coats and fur. Also dispersed in this way, enchanter's nightshade, its small flowers white or pink, has hooked bristles on its club-shaped fruits. Broad-leaved willow-herb, with pale rose flowers, and rose-purple-flowered rosebay willow-herb rely on the wind to spread their plumed seeds. The wind also helps to distribute the small seeds of the foxglove, whose tall stems support numerous drooping flowers of crimson-spotted light purple. This plant lends a touch of stately beauty to the woodland scene, but its other name of dead man's bells reminds us that all its parts are poisonous.

Ferns lack the colour displayed by so many flowering plants, but they, in their individual ways, add considerably to the interest of West Country woods. Bracken, already mentioned as an invader of heath and moor, is quick to find a foothold and sometimes becomes dominant. Polypody, its dark green fronds divided like feathers, occurs on rocks and on the ground, but it attracts more attention when growing on branches and in the forks of oaks and other trees. Lady fern and male fern, members of different genera, are abundant in woods. Broad buckler-fern, a close relative of male fern, is a very variable species, its large fronds triangular or lance-shaped. Soft shield fern has limp drooping leaves, while the dark green mature fronds of hard fern are somewhat leathery. Hart's-tongue fern, as its name suggests, has undivided strap-shaped leaves. Like ferns, pendulous sedge, a species of damp woods, may lack colour, but it has a beauty of its own.

Wall pennywort, also called navelwort, grows on rocks and walls and in damp and shady hedge bottoms.

Very few of the plants referred to are seen in plantations of young conifers once they have reached the 'dense stage' (or, for that matter, in those of immature broad-leaved trees). It is when the trees develop and thinning of the crop takes place that more light reaches the forest floor, permitting the growth of shrubs and smaller plants. Even so, there are usually some interesting plants in open spaces and at the sides of forest tracks and paths. One, the pineapple weed, thrives (and that really is the word!) in the most trampled parts of forest tracks. Also known as rayless chamomile or mayweed, this strongly aromatic herb bears heads of small greenish-yellow flowers. An introduced weed, it is believed to be a native of north-east Asia.

HEDGES AND BANKS

A number of the plants already named in this chapter are among the many species that cover West Country hedges, traditional structures of stone and earth, some of them quite high. Trees and shrubs, their height and form depending largely on the degree of their exposure to wind and salt-spray, may grow on top of these stone hedges. Sheltering beneath them are plants whose colourful blossoms make the region such a joy to flower-lovers in spring and summer.

Primroses are common there and so are bluebells. Herb Robert, a wild geranium, and red campion, with deep pink flowers, also enliven these hedges. Cuckoo pint, also called lords and ladies, is conspicuous in spring, when its large floral sheath opens to reveal part of the fleshy axis around whose lower end the flowers are clustered. It is even more striking when the red berries appear.

Greater stitchwort, weak-stemmed and narrow-leaved, has another name, great starwort, which seems to make an apt comment on its large white flowers. Wall pennywort, often half-hidden by other species, produces spikes of small greenish tubular flowers and fleshy round leaves. The ferns of West Country hedges include such species as polypody, hart's-tongue and hard fern. Grasses and mosses are abundant in these situations and lichens often form patches, some more colourful than others, on exposed stones.

WASTE PLACES

Like the stone hedges, waste places resulting from human activity soon acquire a covering of vegetation. Every part of the region has such areas, but Cornwall, with its old mine and china-clay workings and disused quarries, is especially rich in them. Gorse, blackthorn and ling are important shrubs of general wasteland, while broom and rhododendron are among those playing a useful part by colonizing heaps of waste sand from china-clay workings.

Large numbers of other plants occur in waste places. Early in the year coltsfoot displays its golden yellow flowers, the large leathery leaves appearing later. As the year advances, one sees such tall and familiar species as foxglove and smaller ones like sheep's sorrel, bird's-foot trefoil, its bright yellow flowers with red on the upper petals, and pink-flowered sand spurrey, its stems spreading over china-clay waste and similar material. There are very many more!

The following scientific names of plants mentioned in this chapter are those used in Clapham, Tutin and Warburg's *Excursion Flora* (see Bibliography).

Alder, *Alnus glutinosa*
Alexanders, *Smyrnium olusatrum*
Autumnal squill, *Scilla autumnalis*
Bilberry, *Vaccinium myrtillus*
Bird's-foot trefoil, *Lotus corniculatus*
Biting stonecrop, *Sedum acre*
Blackthorn, *Prunus spinosa*
Bluebell, *Endymion non-scriptus*
Bog asphodel, *Narthecium ossifragum*
Bog myrtle, *Myrica gale*
Bog pimpernel, *Anagallis tenella*
Bog pondweed, *Potamogeton polygonifolius*
Bracken, *Pteridium aquilinum*
Bristle bent-grass, *Agrostis setacea*
Broad buckler-fern, *Dryopteris dilatata*
Broad-leaved willow-herb, *Epilobium montanum*
Broom, *Cytisus scoparius*
Bulbous buttercup, *Ranuculus bulbosus*
Bur-reed, *Sparganium erectum*
Butterbur, *Petasites hybridus*
Butterworts, *Pinguicula lusitanica*, *P. vulgaris*
Canadian pondweed, *Elodea canadensis*
Centaury, *Centaurium erythraea*
Cliff sea-spurrey, *Spergularia rupicola*
Clovers, *Trifolium species*
Coltsfoot, *Tussilago farfara*
Common cotton-grass, *Eriophorum angustifolium*
Common duckweed, *Lemna minor*
Common marsh orchid, *Dactylorhiza praetermissa*
Common reed, *Phragmites australis*
Common rockrose, *Helianthemum nummularium*
Common salt-marsh-grass, *Puccinellia maritima*
Common scurvy-grass, *Cochlearia officinalis*
Common sea lavender, *Limonium vulgare*
Cowslip, *Primula veris*
Creeping buttercup, *Ranunculus repens*
Cross-leaved heath, *Erica tetralix*
Crow garlic, *Allium vineale*
Cuckoo pint, *Arum maculatum*
Curled dock, *Rumex crispus*
Deer-grass, *Trichophorum cespitosum*
Docks, *Rumex species*
Dog's mercury, *Mercurialis perennis*
Early purple orchid, *Orchis mascula*
Enchanter's nightshade, *Circaea lutetiana*
English stonecrop, *Sedum anglicum*
Fescue grasses, *Festuca species*
Foxglove, *Digitalis purpurea*
Gipsy-wort, *Lycopus europaeus*
Gladdon, *Iris foetidissima*
Glasswort, *Salicornia species*
Golden samphire, *Inula crithmoides*
Gorse, *Ulex europaeus*, *U. gallii* (see previous chapter)
Great hairy willow-herb, *Epilobium hirsutum*
Great reedmace, *Typha latifolia*
Greater stitchwort, *Stellaria holostea*
Ground ivy, *Glechoma hederacea*
Hard fern, *Blechnum spicant*
Hare's-tail, *Eriophorum vaginatum*
Hart's-tongue fern, *Phyllitis scolopendrium*
Hazel, *Corylus avellana*
Heath bedstraw, *Galium saxatile*
Heath milkwort, *Polygala serpyllifolia*
Heath spotted orchid, *Dactylorhiza maculata ssp. ericetorum*
Heaths and heathers (see previous chapter)
Herb Robert, *Geranium robertianum*
Himalayan balsam, *Impatiens glandulifera*
Honeysuckle, *Lonicera periclymenum*
Hottentot fig, *Carpobrotus edulis*
Ivy, *Hedera helix*
Knapweed, *Centaurea nigra*
Lady fern, *Athyrium filix-femina*
Lesser celandine, *Ranunculus ficaria*
Ling, *Calluna vulgaris*
Male fern, *Dryopteris filix-mas*
Marram grass, *Ammophila arenaria*
Marsh fleabane, *Pulicaria dysenterica*
Marsh marigold, *Caltha palustris*
Marsh ragwort, *Senecio aquaticus*
Marsh violet, *Viola palustris*
Marsh woundwort, *Stachys palustris*
Mat-grass, *Nardus stricta*
Meadow buttercup, *Ranunculus acris*
Meadowsweet, *Filipendula ulmaria*
Monkey-flower, *Mimulus guttatus*
Moschatel, *Adoxa moschatellina*
Mud rush, *Juncus gerardii*
Pale butterwort, *Pinguicula lusitanica*
Pendulous sedge, *Carex pendula*
Pennywort, *Hydrocotyle vulgaris*
Pineapple weed, *Matricaria matricarioides*
Polypody, *Polypodium vulgare group*
Portland spurge, *Euphorbia portlandica*
Primrose, *Primula vulgaris*
Purple loosestrife, *Lythrum salicaria*
Purple moor-grass, *Molinia caerulea*
Pyramidal orchid, *Anacamptis pyramidalis*
Ragwort, *Senecio jacobaea*
Ramsons, *Allium ursinum*
Red campion, *Silene dioica*
Red fescue, *Festuca rubra*
Reed canary-grass, *Phalaris arundinacea*

Restharrow, *Ononis repens*
Rhododendron, *Rhododendron ponticum*
Ribwort plantain, *Plantago lanceolata*
Rockrose, see Common rockrose, White rockrose
Rock samphire, *Crithmum maritimum*
Rock sea lavender, *Limonium binervosum*
Rosebay willow-herb, *Epilobium angustifolium*
Rushes, *Juncus species*
Salad burnet, *Poterium sanguisorba*
Sallows, Salix species (see Willows in previous chapter)
Sand couch-grass, *Agropyron junceiforme*
Sand spurrey, *Spergularia rubra*
Sea arrow-grass, *Triglochin maritima*
Sea aster, *Aster tripolium*
Sea bindweed, *Calystegia soldanella*
Sea campion, *Silene maritima*
Sea holly, *Eryngium maritimum*
Sea kale, *Crambe maritima*
Sea milkwort, *Glaux maritima*
Sea plantain, *Plantago maritima*
Sea purslane, *Halimione portulacoides*
Sea sandwort, *Honkenya peploides*
Sea spurrey, *Spergularia media, S. marina*
Sedges, *Carex species*
Sheep's-bit, *Jasione montana*
Sheep's sorrel, *Rumex acetosella agg.*
Small scabious, *Scabiosa columbaria*
Soft shield fern, *Polystichum setiferum*
Spring squill, *Scilla verna*
Stemless thistle, *Cirsium acaule*
Sundews, *Drosera species*
Thrift, *Armeria maritima*
Tormentil, *Potentilla erecta*
Townsend's cord-grass, *Spartina x townsendii*
Triquetrous garlic, *Allium triquetrum*
Wall pennywort, *Umbilicus rupestris*
Water figwort, *Scrophularia auriculata*
Water forget-me-nots, *Myosotis species*
Water horsetail, *Equisetum fluviatile*
Water mint, *Mentha aquatica*
Water plantain, *Alisma plantago-aquatica*
Wavy hair-grass, *Deschampsia flexuosa*
White beak-sedge, *Rhynchospora alba*
White rockrose, *Helianthemum apenninum*
Wild carrot, *Daucus carota*
Wild daffodil, *Narcissus pseudonarcissus*
Wild thyme, *Thymus praecox ssp. arcticus*
Willows, Salix species (see previous chapter)
Wood anemone, *Anemone nemorosa*
Wood avens, *Geum urbanum*
Yarrow, *Achillea millefolium*
Yellow flag, *Iris pseudacorus*
Yellow horned poppy, *Glaucium flavum*
Yellow loosestrife, *Lysimachia vulgaris*

Index of West Country birds

Unless otherwise stated, the expression 'breeds' means that species concerned have bred in Somerset, Devon and Cornwall and on Lundy and the Isles of Scilly in recent years. A few species which do not appear to have been sighted in the region during the last twenty years have been omitted.

Accentor, Alpine *Prunella collaris* Extremely rare visitor, Scilly.
Albatross, Black-browed *Diomedea melanophrys* Extremely rare visitor, one offshore Devon, ? one Cornwall.
Auk, Little *Alle alle* Irregular winter visitor to coast. Gale-driven individuals inland.
Avocet *Recurvirostra avosetta* Winter visitor (very local, e.g. on the Exe and the Tamar). Passage birds seen on estuaries and occasionally inland.
Bee-eater *Merops apiaster* Very rare visitor.
Bittern *Botaurus stellaris* Rare winter visitor to dense reed-beds, mainly coast and estuaries. Has bred in Somerset.
——, American *B. lentiginosus* Extremely rare visitor, Cornwall.
——, Little *Ixobrychus minutus* Scarce visitor, mainly in spring.
Blackbird *Turdus merula* Abundant and widespread resident. Breeds. Passage visitor. Winter visitor.
Blackcap *Sylvia atricapilla* Widespread summer visitor. Breeds mainland and Scilly. Small numbers winter here.
Bluethroat *Luscinia svecica* Scarce passage visitor. The red-spotted *L. s. svecica* and white-spotted *L. s. cyanecula* races have been recorded.
Bobolink *Dolichonyx oryzivorus* Extremely rare visitor, Scilly, autumn.
Brambling *Fringilla montifringilla* Winter visitor. Numbers fluctuate considerably. Passage visitor.
Budgerigar *Malopsittacus undulatus* Introduced. Feral population on Tresco, Isles of Scilly. Small flocks seen on several near-by islands.
Bullfinch *Pyrrhula pyrrhula* Common and widespread resident. Breeds throughout mainland, also Tresco. Passage visitor.
Bunting, Black-headed *Emberiza melanocephala* Extremely rare visitor, Scilly, Cornwall.
——, Cirl *E. cirlus* Resident. Breeds locally on mainland. The West Country is one of the few breeding strongholds of the species in Britain.
——, Corn *E. calandra* Resident. Breeds very locally on mainland. Passage visitor.
——, Lapland *Calcarius lapponicus* Scarce passage visitor. Occasionally winters.
——, Little *E. pusilla* Extremely scarce visitor, Scilly, Somerset.
——, Ortolan *E. hortulana* Scarce passage visitor.
——, Reed *E. schoeniclus* Resident. Breeds throughout mainland and on Lundy. Fairly common. Prefers marshes and other wetlands, but also nests some distance from water. Passage visitor. Winter visitor.
——, Rustic *E. rustica* Very rare visitor, Scilly.
——, Snow *Plectrophenax nivalis* Passage visitor. Winter visitor.
——, Yellow-breasted *E. aureola* Very rare visitor, Cornwall and Scilly.
Bustard, Little *Otis tetrax* Extremely rare visitor, Scilly.
Buzzard *Buteo buteo* Resident. Breeds throughout most of the mainland. Passage visitor.
——, Honey *Pernis apivorus* Rare passage visitor.
——, Rough-legged *B. lagopus* Rare visitor.
Chaffinch *Fringilla coelebs* Resident. Breeds. Common, widespread. Winter visitor. Passage visitor.
Chat, Rufous bush *Cercotrichas galactotes* Extremely rare visitor, Devon.
Chiffchaff *Phylloscopus collybita* Summer visitor. Breeds, common, widespread. Passage visitor. A few birds winter here.
Chough *Pyrrhocorax pyrrhocorax* Formerly bred. Individuals reported now are probably 'escapes'.
Coot *Fulica atra* Resident. Breeds locally on mainland and Scilly. Winter visitor to reservoirs and estuaries. Passage visitor.
Cormorant *Phalacrocorax carbo* Resident, numerous. Breeds on coast and Scilly. Visits estuaries, rivers and reservoirs.
Corncrake *Crex crex* Summer visitor. Breeds very locally on mainland and Scilly. Passage visitor.
Courser, Cream-coloured *Cursorius cursor* Very rare visitor, Devon.
Crake, Little *Porzana parva* Very rare visitor.
——, Spotted *P. porzana* An elusive species whose status is far from clear. Breeding suspected in Devon and Somerset in recent years.

Crane *Grus grus* Rare visitor.
Crossbill *Loxia curvirostra* An irruptive migrant which has bred in Devon (and possibly Somerset) in recent years.
——, Two-barred *L. leucoptera* Extremely rare visitor, Lundy.
Crow, European *Corvus corone* Carrion crow *C. c. corone*: abundant and widespread. Resident. Breeds. Hooded crow *C. c. cornix*: occasional visitor.
Cuckoo *Cuculus canorus* Summer visitor, widespread. Breeds.
——, Black-billed *Coccyzus erythrophthalmus* Extremely rare visitor, Lundy and Cornwall.
——, Great Spotted *Clamator glandarius* Extremely rare visitor, Cornwall and Scilly.
——, Yellow-billed *Coccyzus americanus* Extremely rare visitor, Cornwall and Scilly.
Curlew *Numenius arquata* Resident, widespread. Breeds mainland and Lundy. Winter visitor to estuaries. Passage visitor.
——, Stone *Burhinus oedicnemus* Rare visitor.
Dipper *Cinclus cinclus* Resident. Breeds in all three mainland counties, being most widely distributed in Devon.
Diver, Black-throated *Gavia arctica* Winter visitor. Passage visitor.
——, Great Northern *G. immer* Winter visitor, fairly regular. Passage visitor.
——, Red-throated *G. stellata* Winter visitor, usually scarce. Passage visitor.
Dotterel *Eudromias morinellus* Passage visitor, scarce.
Dove, Collared *Streptopelia decaocto* Resident, widespread. Breeds mainland and Scilly.
——, Rock *Columba livia* The wild rock dove was formerly resident. An element of the same species, the feral pigeon, is now widespread, common and breeds.
——, Rufous turtle *S. orientalis* Extremely rare visitor, Cornwall and Scilly.
——, Stock *C. oenas* Resident. Breeds mainland. Widespread. Winter visitor. Passage visitor.
——, Turtle *S. turtur* Summer visitor. Breeds mainly Somerset and Devon. Passage visitor.
Dowitcher, Long-billed *Limnodromus scolopaceus* Very scarce visitor, Somerset, Cornwall, Scilly.
Duck, Black *Anas rubripes* Very rare visitor, Scilly.
——, Ferruginous *Aythya nyroca* Scarce visitor.
——, Long-tailed *Clangula hyemalis* Winter visitor, small numbers.
——, Ring-necked *A. collaris* Rare visitor, Devon, Somerset.
——, Ruddy *Oxyura jamaicensis* Winter visitor, uncommon.
——, Tufted *A. fuligula* Resident. Breeds, mainly in Somerset. Passage visitor. Winter visitor.
Dunlin *Calidris alpina* Resident. A few pairs breed in Devon and possibly also in Cornwall. Winter visitor, some large numbers. Passage visitor.
Dunnock *Prunella modularis* Resident, abundant, widespread. Breeds.
Eagle, White-tailed *Haliaetus albicilla* Very rare visitor, Cornwall.
Egret, Cattle *Bubulcus ibis* Extremely rare visitor (or 'escape'?), Somerset.
——, Little *Egretta garzetta* Rare visitor, spring and autumn.
Eider *Somateria mollissima* Present on tidal waters throughout the year, but more abundant in winter.
Falcon, Gyr *Falco rusticolus* Irregular and scarce visitor.
——, Red-footed *F. vespertinus* Rare visitor.
Fieldfare *Turdus pilaris* Winter visitor, regular. Numbers fluctuate, but some large flocks. Passage visitor.
Firecrest *Regulus ignicapillus* Passage visitor, uncommon. Winter visitor, usually 'singles'.
Flycatcher, Pied *Ficedula hypoleuca* Summer visitor. Breeds on mainland, mainly in Devon and north-west Somerset.
——, Red-breasted *F. parva* Scarce visitor, 'singles' or small numbers.
——, Spotted *Muscicapa striata* Summer visitor. Breeds throughout mainland and on Scilly. Passage visitor.
Fulmar *Fulmarus glacialis* Breeds along mainland coasts (mainly Devon and Cornwall) and on Lundy and Scilly. Present at breeding cliffs January or February to September.
Gadwall *Anas strepera* Feral breeding centres in Scilly (species introduced, 1930s) and Somerset ('escapes' from Wildfowl Trust reserve, Slimbridge). Scarce passage visitor and winter visitor in some other parts of the region.
Gallinule, American purple *Porphyrula martinica* Extremely rare visitor, Scilly.
Gannet *Sula bassana* Seen off coasts, all months.

Garganey *Anas querquedula* Summer visitor, scarce. Breeding irregular, Devon and Somerset. A few winter records. Passage visitor.
Godwit, Bar-tailed *Limosa lapponica* Passage visitor. Common winter visitor. Summer visitor (non-breeding).
——, Black-tailed *L. limosa* Seen all months. Has bred in Somerset. Passage visitor. Winter visitor.
Goldcrest *Regulus regulus* Resident, generally distributed, abundant. Breeds. Passage visitor. Winter visitor.
Goldeneye *Bucephala clangula* Winter visitor. Passage visitor.
Goldfinch *Carduelis carduelis* Resident, widespread. Breeds. Some large autumn/winter flocks.
Goosander *Mergus merganser* Winter visitor, especially during severe weather.
Goose, Barnacle *Branta leucopsis* Winter visitor, rare and irregular.
——, Bean *Anser fabalis* Winter visitor, very rare.
——, Brent *B. bernicla* Winter visitor. Mainly dark-breasted race *B. b. bernicla*.
——, Canada *B. canadensis* Resident. Breeds Devon, Somerset.
——, Greylag *A. anser* Winter visitor, very rare, irregular.
——, Pink-footed *A. brachyrhynchus* Winter visitor, rare, irregular.
——, Red-breasted *B. ruficollis* Very rare visitor ('escape'?), Devon.
——, White-fronted *A. albifrons* Winter visitor, especially in severe weather.
Goshawk *Accipiter gentilis* Scarce visitor.
Grebe, Black-necked *Podiceps nigricollis* Winter visitor, scarce.
——, Great crested *P. cristatus* Resident. Breeds Somerset and Devon. Winter visitor. Passage visitor.
——, Little *Tachybaptus ruficollis* Resident. Breeds locally on mainland. Winter visitor.
——, Red-necked *P. griseigena* Winter visitor, scarce.
——, Slavonian *P. auritus* Winter visitor.
Greenfinch *Carduelis chloris* Resident. Breeds mainland and Scilly. Widespread, common. Winter visitor. Passage visitor.
Greenshank *Tringa nebularia* Passage visitor. Winter visitor.
Grosbeak, Rose-breasted *Pheucticus ludovicianus* Extremely rare visitor, Scilly.
Grouse, Black *Lyrurus tetrix* Resident, very local, scarce. Breeds Exmoor, Dartmoor.
——, Red *Lagopus lagopus* Resident, very local. Breeds Exmoor, Dartmoor.
Guillemot *Uria aalge* Resident. Breeds mainland coast, Lundy, Scilly. Passage visitor. Winter visitor.
——, Black *Cepphus grylle* Winter visitor, rare.
Gull, Black-headed *Larus ridibundus* Has bred Cornwall (exceptional). Winter visitor, common. Passage visitor. Some non-breeders present in summer.
——, Bonaparte's *L. philadelphia* Rare visitor, mainland.
——, Common *L. canus* Winter visitor, abundant. Passage visitor. A few 'summer'.
——, Glaucous *L. hyperboreus* Winter visitor, scarce.
——, Great black-backed *L. marinus* Resident. Breeds. Winter visitor (some very large winter flocks).
——, Herring *L. argentatus* Resident, abundant. Breeds. Winter visitor.
——, Iceland *L. glaucoides* Winter visitor, scarce.
——, Laughing *L. atricilla* Very rare visitor, Scilly, Cornwall.
——, Lesser black-backed *L. fuscus* Migrant. Breeds. Passage visitor. Some overwinter.
——, Little *L. minutus* Passage visitor. Winter visitor. Fairly regular, but uncommon.
——, Mediterranean *L. melanocephalus* Uncommon visitor.
——, Ross's *Rhodostethia rosea* Extremely rare visitor, Cornwall.
——, Sabine's *L. sabini* Passage visitor, scarce.
Harrier, Hen *Circus cyaneus* Winter visitor, rare.
——, Marsh *C. aeruginosus* Passage visitor, rare.
——, Montagu's *C. pygargus* Summer visitor, scarce. Has bred in Cornwall and Devon in recent years. Passage visitor, rare.
Hawfinch *Coccothraustes coccothraustes* An elusive resident. Breeds uncommonly, mostly in Somerset. Also scarce and irregular visitor.
Heron, Grey *Ardea cinerea* Resident, well distributed, locally common. Breeds on mainland. Winter visitor. Passage visitor.
——, Night *Nycticorax nycticorax* Very rare visitor.
——, Purple *A. purpurea* Rare visitor.
——, Squacco *Ardeola ralloides* Very rare visitor.

Hobby *Falco subbuteo* Summer visitor. Breeds on mainland.
Hoopoe *Upupa epops* Mainly scarce passage visitor, but has nested in Cornwall and Somerset in recent years.
Ibis, Glossy *Plegadis falcinellus* Very rare visitor ('escape'?), Devon and Cornwall.
Jackdaw *Corvus monedula* Resident, abundant, widespread. Breeds on mainland. Some large roosts and foraging flocks.
Jay *Garrulus glandarius* Resident, widespread, locally common. Breeds on mainland.
Kestrel *Falco tinnunculus* Resident, widespread, fairly common. Breeds.
——, American *F. sparverius* Extremely rare visitor, Cornwall.
——, Lesser *F. naumanni* Very rare visitor, Cornwall and Scilly.
Killdeer *Charadrius vociferus* Very rare visitor, Scilly.
Kingfisher *Alcedo atthis* Resident, fairly widespread. Breeds on mainland.
Kite, Black *Milvus migrans* Very rare visitor, Scilly and Cornwall.
——, Red *M. milvus* Scarce and irregular visitor. May have bred here in recent years.
Kittiwake *Rissa tridactyla* Present throughout the year. Breeds Cornwall, Devon, Lundy, Scilly.
Knot *Calidris canutus* Common winter visitor and passage visitor. Small numbers (non-breeders) present in summer.
Lapwing *Vanellus vanellus* Widespread resident, locally common. Breeds mainland and Lundy. Abundant winter visitor. Passage visitor.
Lark, Bimaculated *Melanocorypha bimaculata* Extremely rare visitor, Lundy, Scilly.
——, Crested *Galerida cristata* Extremely rare visitor, mainland.
——, Shore *Eremophila alpestris* Scarce visitor.
——, Short-toed *Calandrella cinerea* Very rare visitor, Scilly, Cornwall, Lundy.
Linnet *Acanthis cannabina* Resident, abundant, widespread. Breeds. Winter visitor. Passage visitor.
Magpie *Pica pica* Resident, abundant, widespread. Breeds mainland.
Mallard *Anas platyrhynchos* Resident, widespread. Breeds. Winter visitor, abundant.
Martin, House *Delichon urbica* Summer visitor, common, widespread. Breeds on mainland and Scilly. Passage visitor.
——, Sand *Riparia riparia* Summer visitor, somewhat local, not uncommon. Breeds on mainland and Scilly. Passage visitor.
Merganser, Red-breasted *Mergus serrator* Winter visitor, mainly to Exe estuary, where common.
Merlin *Falco columbarius* Present throughout the year, breeding on Exmoor and possibly in one or two other areas. Local, scarce.
Moorhen *Gallinula chloropus* Resident, abundant, widespread. Breeds on mainland and Scilly. Winter visitor.
Nighthawk *Chordeiles minor* Extremely rare visitor, Scilly.
Nightingale *Luscinia megarhynchos* Summer visitor. Breeds mainly in Somerset, some in Devon, apparently very few or none in Cornwall. Passage visitor.
Nightjar *Caprimulgus europaeus* Summer visitor, somewhat local and scarce. Breeds on mainland. Passage visitor.
Nutcracker *Nucifraga caryocatactes* Irruptive vagrant, mainland and Scilly.
Nuthatch *Sitta europaea* Resident, widespread, fairly common. Breeds on mainland.
Oriole, Baltimore *Icterus galbula* Extremely rare visitor, Scilly, Cornwall, Lundy.
——, Golden *Oriolus oriolus* Scarce and irregular passage visitor.
Osprey *Pandion haliaetus* Scarce passage visitor.
Ouzel, Ring *Turdus torquatus* Summer visitor, scarce. Breeds on mainland, chiefly on high moorland. Passage visitor.
Owl, Barn *Tyto alba* Resident, widely but thinly distributed. Breeds on mainland.
——, Hawk *Surnia ulula* Extremely rare visitor, Cornwall.
——, Little *Athene noctua* Resident, local, not common. Breeds on mainland.
——, Long-eared *Asio otus* Scarce, local. Has bred in Devon and Somerset in recent years. Passage visitor.
——, Scops *Otus scops* Extremely rare visitor, Scilly.
——, Short-eared *A. flammeus* Breeding suspected in Somerset in recent years.
Winter visitor and passage visitor: scarce.
——, Snowy *Nyctea scandiaca* Rare visitor, Devon, Scilly.

——, Tawny *Strix aluco* Resident, widespread, common. Breeds on mainland.

Oystercatcher *Haematopus ostralegus* Resident. Breeds. Winter visitor. Widely distributed along coasts, locally common.

Partridge *Perdix perdix* Resident, widespread, locally fairly common. Breeds on mainland.

——, Red-legged *Alectoris rufa* Resident. Breeds on mainland, locally, mainly in Somerset and Devon.

Parula, Northern *Parula americana* Extremely rare visitor, Cornwall, Scilly.

Peregrine *Falco peregrinus* Resident. Breeds on mainland. Passage visitor. Winter visitor. Some recovery from its dramatic decline.

Petrel, Leach's *Oceanodroma leucorrhoa*. Winter visitor, irregular, mostly as storm vagrant.

——, Storm *Hydrobates pelagicus* Breeds Gulland Rock (Cornwall) and Scilly. Usually seen out to sea, but gales drive some on to coast.

——, Wilson's *Oceanites oceanicus* Extremely rare visitor, Cornwall, autumn.

Phalarope, Grey *Phalaropus fulicarius* Passage visitor, scarce.

——, Red-necked *P. lobatus* Passage visitor, scarce.

——, Wilson's *P. tricolor* Very rare visitor, Cornwall, Scilly, Somerset.

Pheasant *Phasianus colchicus* Resident, widespread, locally common. Breeds.

——, Golden *Chrysolophus pictus* Introduced. Breeds on Scilly.

Pintail *Anas acuta* Winter visitor, locally common. Passage visitor.

Pipit, Meadow *Anthus pratensis* Resident, widespread, locally abundant. Breeds (not Scilly). Winter visitor. Passage visitor.

——, Olive-backed *A. hodgsoni* Extremely rare visitor, Scilly.

——, Red-throated *A. cervinus* Scarce passage visitor, Scilly, Lundy.

——, Richard's *A. novaeseelandiae* Scarce passage visitor, Scilly and mainland (especially Cornwall).

——, Rock/Water *A. spinoletta* Rock pipit *A. s. petrosus*: Resident, quite common. Breeds, coasts. Water pipit *A. s. spinoletta*: Passage visitor. Winter visitor.

——, Tawny *A. campestris* Scarce passage visitor, Scilly and mainland (especially Cornwall).

——, Tree *A. trivialis* Summer visitor, widespread but scarce in places. Breeds on mainland. Passage visitor.

Plover, Golden *Pluvialis apricaria* Resident. Breeds on Dartmoor. Abundant winter visitor and passage visitor.

——, Grey *P. squatarola* Winter visitor and passage visitor, locally common.

——, Kentish *Charadrius alexandrinus* Scarce passage visitor.

——, Lesser golden *P. dominica* Very rare visitor, Scilly, Cornwall, Somerset.

——, Little ringed *C. dubius* Rare passage visitor.

——, Ringed *C. hiaticula* Resident. Breeds on Scilly, very locally on Devon and Somerset coasts. Locally common as passage visitor and winter visitor.

——, Sociable *Vanellus gregarius* Very rare visitor, Devon.

Pochard *Aythya ferina* Breeds Cornwall, Somerset, scarce and local. Winter visitor and passage visitor, locally common.

——, Red-crested *Netta rufina* Scarce visitor.

Pratincole, Collared *Glareola pratincola* Very rare visitor, Cornwall.

——, Black-winged *G. nordmanni* Very rare visitor, Somerset.

Puffin *Fratercula arctica* Summer resident. Breeds on Lundy, Scilly and north Cornish coast. Passage visitor. Storm-vagrant in some areas.

Quail *Coturnix coturnix* Summer visitor, local, irregular. Breeds on mainland and Scilly, sporadically. Passage visitor.

——, Bob-white *Colinus virginianus* Introduced to Tresco, Isles of Scilly, 1964–5, now breeds in the wild.

Rail, Sora *Porzana carolina* Very rare visitor, Scilly.

——, Water *Rallus aquaticus* Resident, local, scarce. Breeds on mainland. Winter visitor and passage visitor, relatively common in places.

Raven *Corvus corax* Resident, widespread, especially in Cornwall and Devon. Breeds on mainland and Lundy. Fairly common in places.

Razorbill *Alca torda* Resident, locally quite common. Breeds on Lundy, Scilly and mainland coasts (particularly Cornwall).

Redpoll *Acanthis flammea* Resident. Breeds on mainland, mainly in Devon. Passage visitor. Winter visitor. Mealy redpoll *A. f. flammea*: very rare visitor. Greenland redpoll *A. f. rostrata*: has been recorded in Scilly.

——, Arctic *A. hornemanni* Extremely rare visitor, Scilly.

Redshank *Tringa totanus* Resident. Breeds on mainland, mainly Somerset. Passage visitor and winter visitor, locally common.
——, Spotted *T. erythropus* Passage visitor and winter visitor, regular.
Redstart *Phoenicurus phoenicurus* Summer visitor, regular, widely but unevenly distributed. Breeds on mainland. Passage visitor.
——, American *Setophaga ruticilla* Extremely rare visitor, Cornwall.
——, Black *Phoenicurus ochruros* Passage visitor and winter visitor, regular but scarce.
Redwing *Turdus iliacus* Winter visitor and passage visitor, common.
Robin *Erithacus rubecula* Resident, abundant, widespread. Breeds. Passage visitor. Winter visitor.
——, American *Turdus migratorius* Very rare visitor, Scilly, Lundy.
Roller *Coracias garrulus* Rare visitor, mainland and Scilly.
Rook *Corvus frugilegus* Resident, abundant, widespread. Breeds on mainland.
Rosefinch, Scarlet *Carpodacus erythrinus* Very rare visitor, Scilly, Lundy, Somerset.
Ruff *Philomachus pugnax* Winter visitor and passage visitor.
Sanderling *Calidris alba* Winter visitor, passage visitor and non-breeding summer visitor. Relatively common in places.
Sandpiper, Baird's *C. bairdii* Rare visitor, Somerset, Cornwall, Scilly and Lundy.
——, Broad-billed *Limicola falcinellus* Rare visitor, Devon, Somerset.
——, Buff-breasted *Tryngites subruficollis* Rare visitor, Lundy, Scilly and mainland.
——, Common *Actitis hypoleucos* Summer visitor. Breeding uncommon, very local on mainland. Winter visitor. Passage visitor.
——, Curlew *Calidris ferruginea* Passage visitor, uncommon.
——, Green *Tringa ochropus* Passage visitor, regular. Winter visitor.
——, Least *C. minutilla* Very rare visitor, Devon, Cornwall, Scilly.
——, Pectoral *C. melanotos* Very rare visitor, mainland, Lundy, Scilly.
——, Purple *C. maritima* Passage visitor and winter visitor, numbers usually small.
——, Semi-palmated *C. pusillus* Very rare visitor, Lundy and Scilly.
——, Sharp-tailed *C. acuminata* Very rare visitor, Scilly.
——, Solitary *T. solitaria* Very rare visitor, Scilly.
——, Spotted *A. macularia* Very rare visitor, Cornwall, Somerset and Scilly.
——, Terek *Xenus cinereus* Very rare visitor, mainland.
——, Upland *Bartramia longicauda* Very rare visitor, Cornwall, Scilly.
——, Western *C. mauri* Very rare visitor, Devon.
——, White-rumped *C. fuscicollis* Very rare visitor, mainland, Scilly.
——, Wood *T. glareola* Passage visitor, scarce.
Sapsucker, Yellow-bellied *Sphyrapicus varius* Extremely rare visitor, Tresco, Isles of Scilly.
Scaup *Aythya marila* Winter visitor and passage visitor, scarce.
Scoter, Common *Melanitta nigra* Winter visitor, passage visitor and non-breeding summer visitor. Numbers and movements irregular.
——, Surf *M. perspicillata* Extremely rare visitor, Devon, Scilly.
——, Velvet *M. fusca* Winter visitor, scarce, regular in places.
Serin *Serinus serinus* Very rare visitor.
Shag *Phalacrocorax aristotelis* Resident, common. Breeds on mainland coasts (mainly Cornwall and Devon), Lundy and Scilly.
Shearwater, Cory's *Calonectris diomedea* Extremely scarce visitor, Cornwall, Scilly, Devon.
——, Great *Puffinus gravis* Passage visitor.
——, Little *P. assimilis* Extremely scarce visitor, Cornwall, Scilly.
——, Manx *P. puffinus* Summer visitor. Breeds Scilly, Lundy. Passage visitor.
——, Sooty *P. griseus* Passage visitor.
Shelduck *Tadorna tadorna* Resident, locally common. Breeds on mainland and Scilly. Winter visitor.
——, Ruddy *T. ferruginea* Very rare visitor ('escape'?), Cornwall, Somerset.
Shoveler *Anas clypeata* Breeds: uncommon, mainland (Devon and Somerset), Scilly. Winter visitor. Passage visitor.
Shrike, Great grey *Lanius excubitor* Passage visitor, winter visitor, irregular, scarce.
——, Lesser grey *L. minor* Very rare visitor, Cornwall, Lundy, Somerset.
——, Red-backed *L. collurio* Summer visitor, local, scarce. Breeds on mainland (few localities). Passage visitor.
——, Woodchat *L. senator* Passage visitor, scarce, irregular.

Siskin *Carduelis spinus* Resident. Breeds in Devon. Winter visitor. Passage visitor.

Skua, Arctic *Stercorarius parasiticus* Passage visitor. Winter visitor.

——, Great *S. skua* Passage visitor. Winter visitor.

——, Long-tailed *S. longicaudus* Very rare visitor.

——, Pomarine *S. pomarinus* Passage visitor, uncommon.

Skylark *Alauda arvensis* Resident, abundant, widespread. Breeds. Common winter visitor and passage visitor.

Smew *Mergus albellus* Winter visitor, somewhat irregular, local, scarce.

Snipe *Gallinago gallinago* Resident, local. Breeds on mainland. Winter visitor and passage visitor, locally common.

——, Great *G. media* Very rare visitor, Scilly.

——, Jack *Lymnocryptes minima* Winter visitor and passage visitor, widespread, scarce.

Sparrow, House *Passer domesticus* Resident, widespread, abundant. Breeds.

——, Spanish *P. hispaniolensis* Extremely rare visitor, Lundy, Scilly.

——, Tree *P. montanus* Resident, local. Breeds on mainland (mainly Somerset). Winter visitor. Passage visitor.

Sparrowhawk *Accipiter nisus* Resident, widespread, locally fairly common. Breeds on mainland. Passage visitor.

Spoonbill *Platalea leucorodia* Irregular and scarce visitor, estuaries.

Starling *Sturnus vulgaris* Resident, widespread, abundant. Breeds. Winter visitor. Passage visitor.

——, Rose-coloured *S. roseus* Very rare visitor.

Stilt, Black-winged *Himantopus himantopus* Very rare visitor, mainland.

Stint, Little *Calidris minuta* Passage visitor, numbers usually small. Occasionally winters.

——, Temminck's *C. temminckii* Very rare visitor.

Stonechat *Saxicola torquata* Resident, common, widespread. Breeds on mainland and Scilly.

Stork, Black *Ciconia nigra* Extremely rare visitor, Cornwall.

——, White *C. ciconia* Very rare visitor.

Swallow *Hirundo rustica* Summer visitor, widespread, common. Breeds. Passage visitor, abundant.

——, Red-rumped *H. daurica* Very rare visitor, Devon, Scilly, Cornwall.

Swan, Bewick's *Cygnus bewickii* Winter visitor, numbers variable (greatest in severe weather). Also passage visitor, occasional.

——, Mute *C. olor* Resident, locally common. Breeds on mainland and Scilly. Winter visitor.

——, Whooper *C. cygnus* Winter visitor, scarce, very local. Passage visitor, occasional.

Swift *Apus apus* Summer visitor, widespread, abundant. Breeds on mainland and Scilly. Passage visitor.

——, Alpine *A. melba* Very rare visitor, mainland, Lundy, Scilly.

Tanager, Scarlet *Piranga olivacea* Extremely rare visitor, Scilly.

Teal *Anas crecca* Resident. Breeds very locally and irregularly on mainland and Scilly. Winter visitor, locally common. Passage visitor. The green-winged teal *A. c. carolinensis* occurs as a vagrant.

——, Blue-winged *A. discors* Extremely rare visitor, Cornwall, Scilly.

Tern, Arctic *Sterna paradisaea* Passage visitor. Breeds Scilly.

——, Black *Chlidonias niger* Passage visitor, local.

——, Caspian *Hydroprogne caspia* Very rare visitor, Devon, Somerset.

——, Common *S. hirundo* Summer visitor. Breeds on Scilly. Passage visitor, regular.

——, Gull-billed *Gelochelidon nilotica* Very rare visitor, Devon, Cornwall, Scilly.

——, Little *S. albifrons* Passage visitor, regular, small numbers.

——, Roseate *S. dougallii* Summer visitor. Breeds on Scilly. Passage visitor, scarce.

——, Royal *S. maxima* Extremely rare visitor, Cornwall.

——, Sandwich *S. sandvicensis* Passage visitor, relatively common.

——, Whiskered *Chlidonias hybrida* Rare visitor, mainland.

——, White-winged black *C. leucopterus* Rare visitor, mainland, Scilly.

Thrush, Eye-browed *Turdus obscurus* Extremely rare visitor, Scilly.

——, Grey-cheeked *Catharus minimus* Extremely rare visitor, Scilly and Cornwall.

——, Mistle *T. viscivorus* Resident, widespread, common. Breeds on mainland. Passage visitor. Winter visitor.

——, Rock *Monticola saxatilis* Extremely rare visitor, Cornwall (Eddystone).

——, Song *T. philomelos* Resident, widespread, common. Breeds on mainland and Scilly. Winter visitor. Passage visitor.
Tit, Bearded *Panurus biarmicus* Winter visitor, almost regular.
——, Blue *Parus caeruleus* Resident, widespread, abundant. Breeds on mainland and Scilly. Passage visitor. Winter visitor.
——, Coal *P. ater* Resident, widespread, common. Breeds on mainland and Scilly. Passage visitor. Winter visitor.
——, Crested *P. cristatus* Vagrant.
——, Great P. major Resident, widespread, abundant. Breeds on mainland and Scilly. Passage visitor.
——, Long-tailed *Aegithalos caudatus* Resident, widespread, abundant. Breeds on mainland.
——, Marsh *P. palustris* Resident, widespread, common. Breeds on mainland.
——, Willow *P. montanus* Resident. Breeds on mainland. Confused with the marsh tit.
Towhee, Rufous-sided *Pipilo erythrophthalmus* Extremely rare visitor, Lundy.
Treecreeper *Certhia familiaris* Resident, widespread, common. Breeds on mainland.
Turnstone *Arenaria interpres* Passage visitor. Winter visitor, relatively common, local. Summer visitor (non-breeding).
Twite *Acanthis flavirostris* Vagrant.
Veery *Catharus fuscescens* Extremely rare visitor, Cornwall.
Vireo, Red-eyed *Vireo olivaceous* Vagrant, Scilly.
Wagtail, Grey *Motacilla cinerea* Resident, widespread, common. Breeds on mainland. Winter visitor. Passage visitor.
——, Pied/White *M. alba* Pied wagtail *M. a. yarrellii*: Resident, widespread, common. Breeds on mainland, Lundy, Scilly. Passage visitor. Winter visitor. White wagtail *M. a. alba*: Passage visitor.
——, Yellow/Blue-headed *M. flava* Yellow wagtail *M. f. flavissima*: Summer visitor, local. Breeds on mainland, particularly in south Devon and Somerset. Passage visitor, common. Blue-headed wagtail *M. f. flava*: Passage visitor, scarce, irregular.
Wallcreeper *Tichodroma muraria* Extremely rare visitor, Somerset.
Warbler, Aquatic *Acrocephalus paludicola* Passage visitor, scarce, mainland, Scilly.
——, Arctic *Phylloscopus borealis* Very rare visitor, Scilly, Lundy, Somerset.
——, Barred *Sylvia nisoria* Scarce passage visitor.
——, Black-and-white *Mniotilta varia* Vagrant, Scilly.
——, Blackpoll *Dendroica striata* Vagrant, Scilly, Devon.
——, Bonelli's *P. bonelli* Very rare visitor, Cornwall, Scilly, Lundy.
——, Booted *Hippolais caligata* Extremely rare visitor, Scilly.
——, Cetti's *Cettia cetti* Resident. Breeds in Devon. Also recorded in Cornwall and Somerset. Numbers small.
——, Dartford *S. undata* Resident, very local, scarce. Breeds in Devon.
——, Dusky *P. fuscatus* Extremely rare visitor, Scilly.
——, Garden *S. borin* Summer visitor, widespread. Breeds on mainland. Passage visitor.
——, Grasshopper *Locustella naevia* Summer visitor, widespread. Breeds on mainland. Passage visitor.
——, Great reed *A. arundinaceus* Rare visitor, mainland, Scilly.
——, Greenish *P. trochiloides* Rare visitor, Lundy, Scilly.
——, Hooded *Wilsonia citrina* Extremely rare visitor, Scilly.
——, Icterine *H. icterina* Passage visitor, scarce.
——, Marsh *A. palustris* Summer visitor, extremely local, very scarce. Breeds in Somerset.
——, Melodious *H. polyglotta* Passage visitor, scarce.
——, Myrtle *D. coronata* Extremely rare visitor, Lundy, Scilly.
——, Olivaceous, *H. pallida* Extremely rare visitor, Cornwall, Scilly.
——, Orphean *S. hortensis* Extremely rare visitor, Cornwall.
——, Paddyfield *A. agricola* Extremely rare visitor, Scilly.
——, Pallas's *P. proregulus* Very rare visitor, Cornwall, Scilly.
——, Radde's *P. schwarzi* Extremely rare visitor, Scilly.
——, Reed *A. scirpaceus* Summer visitor. Breeds on mainland, Scilly. Passage visitor.
——, Savi's *L. luscinioides* Rare visitor.
——, Sedge *A. schoenobaenus* Summer visitor, local, fairly common in places. Breeds on mainland and Scilly. Passage visitor.

——, Spectacled *S. conspicillata* Extremely rare visitor, Cornwall.
——, Subalpine *S. cantillans* Very rare visitor, Devon, Scilly, Cornwall.
——, Willow *P. trochilus* Summer visitor, widespread, abundant. Breeds. Passage visitor.
——, Wood *P. sibilatrix* Summer visitor, widespread in Devon, somewhat local elsewhere. Breeds on mainland. Passage visitor.
——, Yellow-browed *P. inornatus* Passage visitor, rare. Cornwall, Devon, Scilly.
Waterthrush, Northern *Seiurus noveboracensis* Extremely rare visitor, Scilly.
Waxwing *Bombycilla garrulus* Winter visitor, irregular.
Wheatear *Oenanthe oenanthe* Summer visitor, local, two strongholds being Dartmoor and Exmoor. Breeds on mainland and Lundy. Passage visitor, common.
——, Black-eared *O. hispanica* Very rare visitor, Scilly, Cornwall.
——, Desert *O. deserti* Very rare visitor, Scilly.
——, Isabelline *O. isabellina* Very rare visitor, Scilly.
Whimbrel *Numenius phaeopus* Passage visitor, regular, common. Occasional summering and wintering birds.
Whinchat *Saxicola rubetra* Summer visitor, locally common. Breeds on mainland. Passage visitor.
Whitethroat *Sylvia communis* Summer visitor, widespread. Breeds on mainland, Scilly and Lundy. Passage visitor.
——, Lesser *S. curruca* Summer visitor, local. Breeds on mainland. Passage visitor.
Wigeon *Anas penelope* Winter visitor, abundant. Occasional summering individuals.
——, American *A. americana* Very rare visitor, Somerset, Scilly.
Woodcock *Scolopax rusticola* Breeds Devon and Somerset. Winter visitor and passage visitor, locally common some years.
Woodlark *Lullula arborea* Resident, very local, scarce. Breeds on mainland.
Woodpecker, Great spotted *Dendrocopos major* Resident, widespread, fairly common. Breeds on mainland.
——, Green *Picus viridis* Resident, widespread, common. Breeds on mainland.
——, Lesser spotted *D. minor* Resident, local. Breeds on mainland.
Woodpigeon *Columba palumbus* Resident, widespread, abundant. Breeds. Winter visitor.
Wren *Troglodytes troglodytes* Resident, widespread, abundant. Breeds.
Wryneck *Jynx torquilla* Passage visitor, scarce. May have bred recently.
Yellowhammer *Emberiza citrinella* Resident, widespread, abundant. Breeds.
Yellowlegs, Greater *Tringa melanoleuca* Extremely rare visitor, Scilly.
——, Lesser *T. flavipes* Very rare visitor, mainland and Scilly.

Nature reserves and other places to visit

This section should be used in conjunction with the map and the Bibliography. There are several other nature reserves, but details of their locations are restricted to members of the organizations controlling them.

CORNWALL

1 (*This number is used on the map to indicate an approximate position.*) Cardinham Woods, near Bodmin. *O.S. Grid Ref.* 099 665 Walks and trails, 1½–3½m. Forestry Commission leaflet.

2 Coombe Valley, near Bude. 210 117 Nature trail, 1½m. Forestry Commission booklet.

3 Cotehele, 2m. west of Gunnislake. 424 681 Woodland walk, 1½m. (See National Trust booklet *Country Walks in Devon and Cornwall.*)

4 Deer Park Wood, near Liskeard. 198 604 Forest trail, 2m. Forestry Commission leaflet.

5 Halvana Plantations, near Five Lanes (A30, Launceston to Bodmin). 213 788 Forest trail, 1½m. Forestry Commission leaflet.

6 Lanhydrock, 2½m. south of Bodmin. 085 636 Access on foot to park and woods at all times. (See National Trust booklet *Country Walks in Devon and Cornwall.*)

7 Mount Edgcumbe, west of Plymouth. 408 511–455 533 Country Park.

8 Shute Wood, St Agnes. 742 522 Small deciduous wood. Woodland Trust.

9 Trelissick, 4m. south of Truro. 830 397 Woodland trail, 1½–2m. (See National Trust booklet *Country Walks in Devon and Cornwall.*)

10 Trengwainton, 2m. west of Penzance. 445 315 National Trust gardens (Birds).

DEVON

11 Abbeyford Woods, near Okehampton. 589 973 Forest walks, 1½–2½m. (See Forestry Commission booklet *See Halwill Forest.*)

12 Arlington Court, 7m. north-east of Barnstaple. 611 405 Nature trail: woodland and lakeside. National Trust.

13 Ashculm Turbary, Hemyock. 147 158 Nature reserve, 16 acres. Devon Trust for Nature Conservation.

14 Ash Hill, Ottery St Mary. 065 927 Beech woodland, 1·8 acres. Devon Trust for Nature Conservation.

15 Avon Valley Woods, near Kingsbridge. 732 486 Loddiswell, 736 509 Bedlime: Woodland, 100 acres, stretching for almost two miles along the east bank of the river Avon from Loddiswell station to Hendham Cross. Woodland Trust.

16 Axmouth–Lyme Regis Undercliffs National Nature Reserve. 290 897 Public footpath along length of this 800-acre reserve (Underhill Farm near Lyme Regis to Bindon Cliff). Visitors must not leave this path without a written permit from Nature Conservancy Council regional office. NCC leaflet.

17 Bellever Woodlands, Dartmoor. 656 761 Forest walks, 1½–3½m. Forestry Commission booklet.

18 Berry Head, ½m. east of Brixham. 941 565 Country Park, limestone headland.

19 Blackadon, Leusdon. 712 732 Nature reserve, 90 acres. Devon Trust for Nature Conservation.

20 Black Tor Copse, 4m. north-east of Lydford. 567 890 Forest nature reserve. Nature Conservancy Council.

21 Bolberry Down, near Salcombe. 688 385 Coastal walk, 1m. (See National Trust booklet *Country Walks in Devon and Cornwall.*)

22 Bovey Valley Woodlands National Nature Reserve, 4m. north-west of Bovey Tracey. Nature Conservancy Council. Permit required to visit parts away from public footpaths.

23 Braunton Burrows National Nature Reserve, north-west of Barnstaple. 450 350 Sand-dune reserve. Boarded footpath. Nature Conservancy Council leaflet.

24 Bridford Wood, 3m. north-east of Moretonhampstead. Oak-covered hillside, 84 acres. Woodland walks. National Trust.

25 Buck's Wood, Buck's Mills. 355 234 Valley woodland, 5 acres. Woodland Trust.

26 Cairn Top, Ilfracombe. 515 463 Nature reserve, 19 acres. Devon Trust for Nature Conservation.

27 Charleton Footpath Trail, near Kingsbridge. 7552 4263 Kingsbridge estuary trail. (See *Devon Wetlands* (comp. Hunt and Wills).)

28 Chudleigh Knighton Heath. 838 776 Nature reserve, 180 acres. Devon Trust for Nature Conservation.

29 Cleaveland Wood, near Bere Alston. 437 651 Mixed wood, 4½ acres. Woodland Trust.

30 Cowley Cleave Nature Trail, 1½m. west of Parracombe. 645 445 Woodland, mixed farmland, riverside walk, ¾m. Guide available at site.

31 Crowndale Wood, near Tavistock. 474 734 Mature trees along the bank of the Tavistock Canal, 2½ acres. Walk. Woodland Trust.
32 Dart Valley. Dartmeet 672 733 S. end 704 704 Nature reserve, 900 acres. Devon Trust for Nature Conservation.
33 Dunsford and Meadhaydown Wood, 9m. west of Exeter. 805 883 Nature reserve, 140 acres. Devon Trust for Nature Conservation pamphlet.
34 Eggesford Forest, ½m. south of Eggesford station. Forest walks, ¾m. Forestry Commission booklet.
35 Farway Countryside Park, 4m. south of Honiton. 187 932 Country Park: wood, heath and meadowland.
36 Hangingcliff Wood, Bere Ferrers. 425 665 Nature reserve, 7½ acres. Devon Trust for Nature Conservation.
37 Hardwick Wood, Plymouth. 528 554 48-acre wood, walks. Woodland Trust.
38 Heddon Valley, 4m. west of Lynton. 653 482 Nature trail, 2m. Guide on sale at Hunter's Inn Hotel.
39 Hembury Woods, 2m. north of Buckfastleigh. 730 680 Woodland walk, 1½m. (See National Trust booklet *Country Walks in Devon and Cornwall.*)
40 Holsworthy Woods, 1½m. south of Holsworthy. 353 014 Forest Walk, 1m. (See Forestry Commission booklet *See Halwill Forest.*)
41 Lady's Wood, South Brent. 686 591 Nature reserve, 8 acres. Devon Trust for Nature Conservation.
42 Lickham Common, Hemyock. 126 122 Nature reserve, 10 acres. Devon Trust for Nature Conservation.
43 Lydford Gorge, Half-way between Okehampton and Tavistock. 509 846 Riverside walk. National Trust.
44 Lydford Woods. 501 852 Forest trail, 2m. (See Forestry Commission booklet *See Halwill Forest.*)
45 Morwellham Blue Trail, 4m. west of Tavistock. Canal with tunnel, 2m. Guide on sale at Morwellham Quay Centre.
46 Page Wood, Sidmouth. 137 879 small wood, 1 acre. Woodland Trust.
47 The Pinetum, Uplyme. Lyme Regis. 317 935 Arboretum and wood, 7 acres. Woodland Trust.
48 Plym Forest, near Plym Bridge. 537 595 Forest trail, 1¼m. Forestry Commission leaflet.
49 Rectory Field, East Ogwell. 842 696 Wooded pasture, 5½ acres. Woodland Trust.
50 Salcombe Plantation. 735 385 Small wood. Woodland Trust.
51 Shaptor Woods, Bovey Tracey. 819 798 Little John's Walk; 809 808 Shaptor Rock; 807 808 Wooded valley, 200 acres, with footpaths and circular walk. Woodland Trust.
52 Sidmouth Cliff. Dunscombe Cliff 150 878; Salcombe Hill Cliff 133 874 Nature reserve, 18·6 acres. Nature trail (Devon Trust for Nature Conservation booklet) at Salcombe Hill.
53 Slapton Ley. 828 444; 823 423 Nature trails: Slapton Ley footpath, 1½m. Slapton Sands footpath, 3m. Guides on sale at Slapton Ley Field Centre.
54 Snakey Copse, Kingskerswell. 874 675 Small wood, 1 acre (perimeter path). Woodland Trust.
55 South Plantation, Sheldon. 114 094 Mixed woodland, 30 acres. Woodland Trust.
56 Stoke Woods, on A396 Exeter to Tiverton road. 920 960 Forest walks, ½-1½m. Forestry Commission booklet.
57 Tod Moor, Westlake. 625 540 Nature reserve, 17 acres. Devon Trust for Nature Conservation.
58 Trowlesworthy Warren. 565 645 Moorland and woodland walk, 2m. (See National Trust booklet *Country Walks in Devon and Cornwall.*)
59 Westcott Wood, Moretonhampstead. 785 873 Small wood, 13 acres. Woodland Trust.
60 Wistman's Wood, 2½m. north-east of Princetown. Forest nature reserve. Nature Conservancy Council.
61 Wolborough, Newton Abbot. 866 703 Nature reserve, 13 acres. Devon Trust for Nature Conservation.
62 Yarner Wood National Nature Reserve, 2m. west of Bovey Tracey. 784 787 Woodland and heath. Nature trail, 1½m. Woodland walk, 3m. Nature Conservancy Council guides on sale.

LUNDY 63

Unspoilt island in Bristol Channel, 22m. from Ilfracombe. Owned by National Trust, leased to the Landmark Trust. Steamers: May to end of September, P. & A. Campbell Ltd., 10 The Quay, Ilfracombe (landing not always possible). Lundy Field Society arranges an annual excursion and courses on the island.

SCILLY, ISLES OF 64
See P. Z. Mackenzie's booklet *The Isles of Scilly: nature trails and wildlife conservation* for details of Lower Moors, Higher Moors and Holy Vale trails and other features of interest.

SOMERSET
65 Berrow Dunes, near Burnham-on-Sea. 293 541 Sand-dunes. Booklet available from Somerset Trust for Nature Conservation.
66 Biddle Combe, 2m. north-east of Wells. 569 489 Nature trail, 2½m. Guide on sale at Wells museum.
67 Black Rock Nature Reserve, head of Cheddar Gorge. 486 548 Nature trails, 1½ and 4m. Somerset Trust for Nature Conservation leaflet.
68 Brean Down, 2m. south-west of Weston-super-Mare. 297 587 Mendip extension. Somerset Trust for Nature Conservation booklet.
69 Cloutsham, Webber's Post car park, Exmoor. 903 438 Nature trail, 3m. Booklet from National Trust and Exmoor National Park Information Centres.
70 Ebbor Gorge National Nature Reserve, Wookey, near Wells. 521 484 Mendip woodland trails, ½–1½m. Nature Conservancy Council leaflet.
71 Fyne Court, Broomfield. 222 322 Headquarters of Somerset Trust for Nature Conservation. Woodland walks. Guide on sale.
72 Long Wood Reserve, off the Cheddar Gorge road. 488 551 Nature trail. Somerset Trust for Nature Conservation leaflet.
73 Moors Trail, near Wells on A371, Easton church to Wookey. Nature trail, 4m. Booklet on sale at Wells museum.
74 Neroche Forest, Castle Neroche, near Staple Fitzpaine. 274 157 Forest trail, 2m. Forestry Commission booklet.
75 North Hill, Minehead. 969 473 Nature trail, 3m. Booklet from National Trust and Exmoor National Park Information Centres.
76 Quantock Forest, Seven Wells Bridge, Nether Stowey. 173 373 Forest trail, 2½m. Forestry Commission booklet.
77 Wells. Nature trail, 2½–3m., from Market Square. Fields and woodlands. Booklet on sale at Wells museum.

STEEP HOLM 78
Island nature reserve, 5m. off Weston-super-Mare. Restricted visiting, *via* Weston-super-Mare, April–October. Day trips (Saturdays only), weekly visits (Saturday to Saturday), and weekends (across Saturday, return either Sunday or Monday). Details from Kenneth Allsop Memorial Trust.

GUIDED WALKS
Dartmoor: Easter–September, walks of various lengths. September–Easter, walks of four hours at weekends. Small charge made. Details from National Park Information Centres or Dartmoor National Park Department, Guided Walks Centre, Courtenay House, Fore Street, Bovey Tracey. Exmoor: Late March–September, walks of various lengths. Small charge made. Details from National Park Information Centres or Exmoor National Park Office, Exmoor House, Dulverton, Somerset.

CORNWALL and the Isles of Scilly

The numbers in bold type indicate locations of Nature Reserves and other places to visit listed on pages 141–143

Built up areas

'A' roads   'B' roads

Note: When planning routes, the reader is advised to consult a large scale road map or Bartholomew's 1:100,000 maps, nos. 1, 2 & 3

0 5 10 15 km
0 5 10 miles

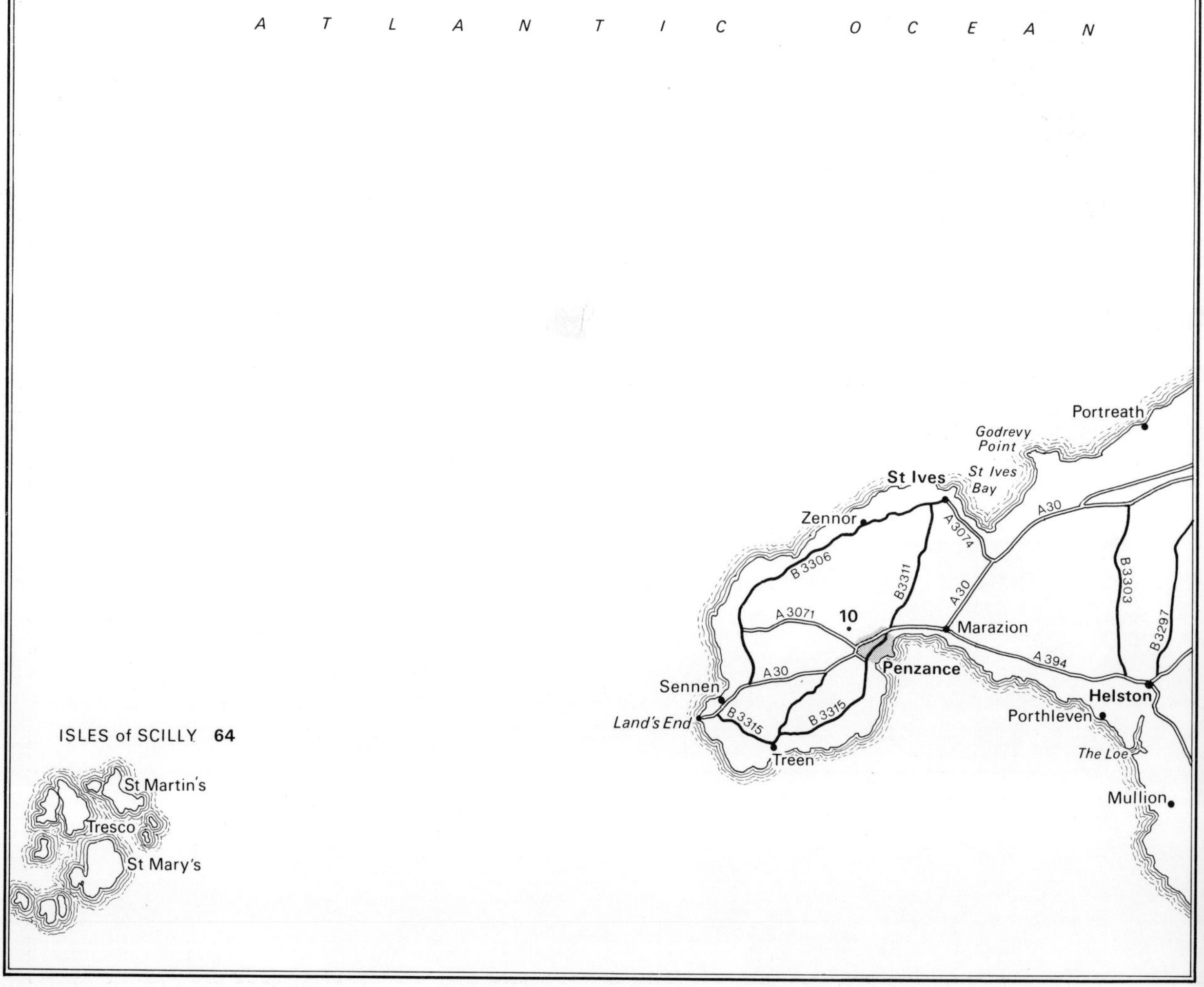

A T L A N T I C   O C E A N

ISLES of SCILLY **64**

St Martin's
Tresco
St Mary's

Portreath
Godrevy Point
St Ives
St Ives Bay
Zennor
A 3074
A 30
B 3306
B 3311
B 3303
A 3071
10
Marazion
B 3297
A 394
Penzance
A 30
Sennen
Helston
Land's End
B 3315
B 3315
Porthleven
Treen
The Loe
Mullion

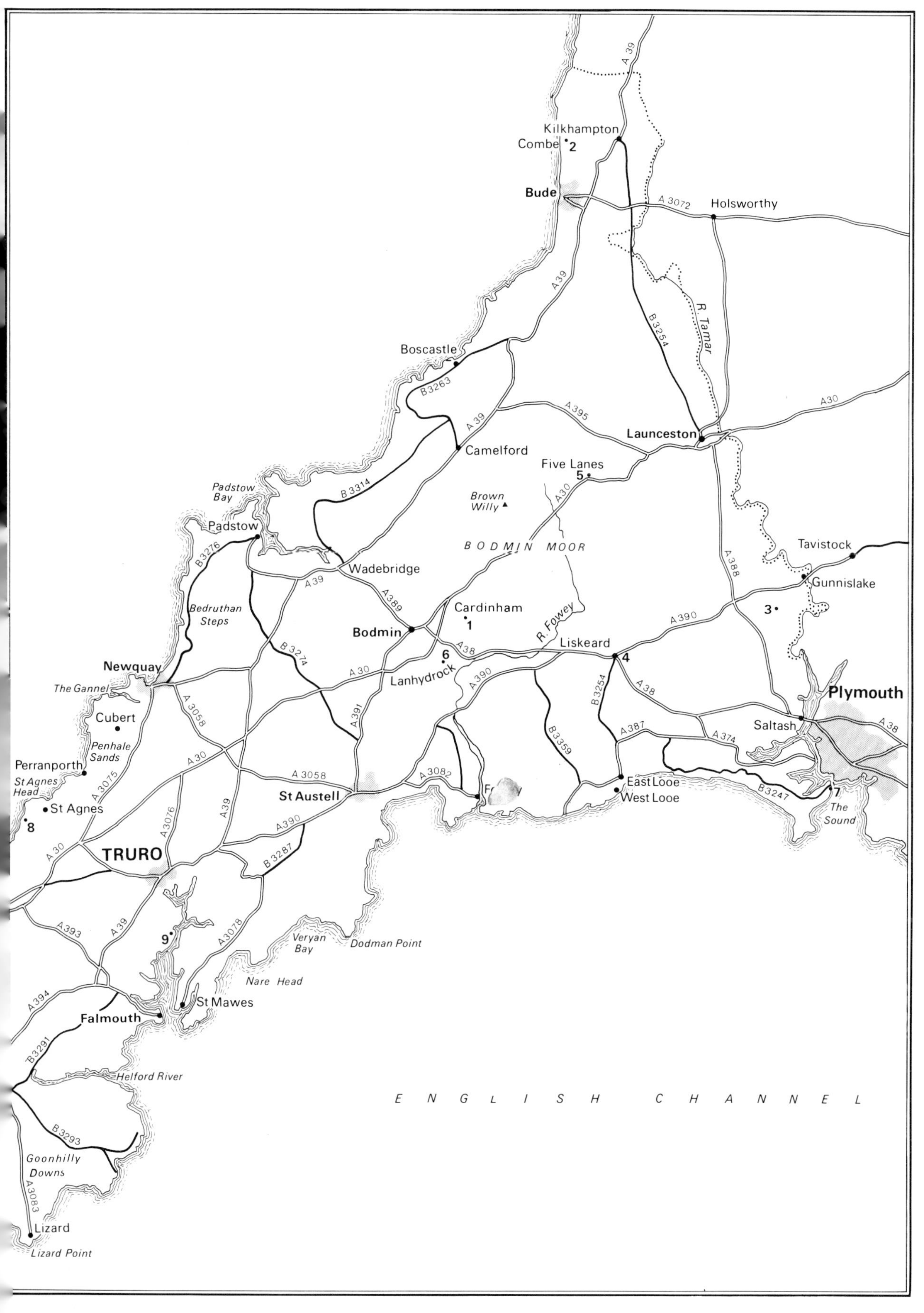

Kilkhampton
Combe
2
Bude
A 3072
Holsworthy
A 39
R. Tamar
B 3254
Boscastle
B 3263
A 39
A 395
A 30
Launceston
Camelford
Five Lanes
5
Padstow Bay
B 3314
Brown Willy
A 30
Padstow
BODMIN MOOR
Tavistock
B 3276
Wadebridge
Gunnislake
A 39
A 388
A 389
Cardinham
1
3
Bedruthan Steps
R. Fowey
A 390
Bodmin
Liskeard
B 3274
6
A 38
4
Newquay
A 30
Lanhydrock
A 390
Plymouth
The Gannel
A 38
B 3254
A 3058
Cubert
A 391
Saltash
A 387
A 374
A 38
Penhale Sands
B 3359
A 30
Perranporth
A 3058
A 3082
East Looe
St Agnes Head
A 3075
St Austell
West Looe
B 3247
7
St Agnes
A 3076
A 39
The Sound
8
A 390
A 30
TRURO
B 3287
A 393
A 39
A 3078
9
Veryan Bay
Dodman Point
Nare Head
A 394
St Mawes
Falmouth
B 3291
Helford River
ENGLISH CHANNEL
B 3293
Goonhilly Downs
A 3083
Lizard
Lizard Point

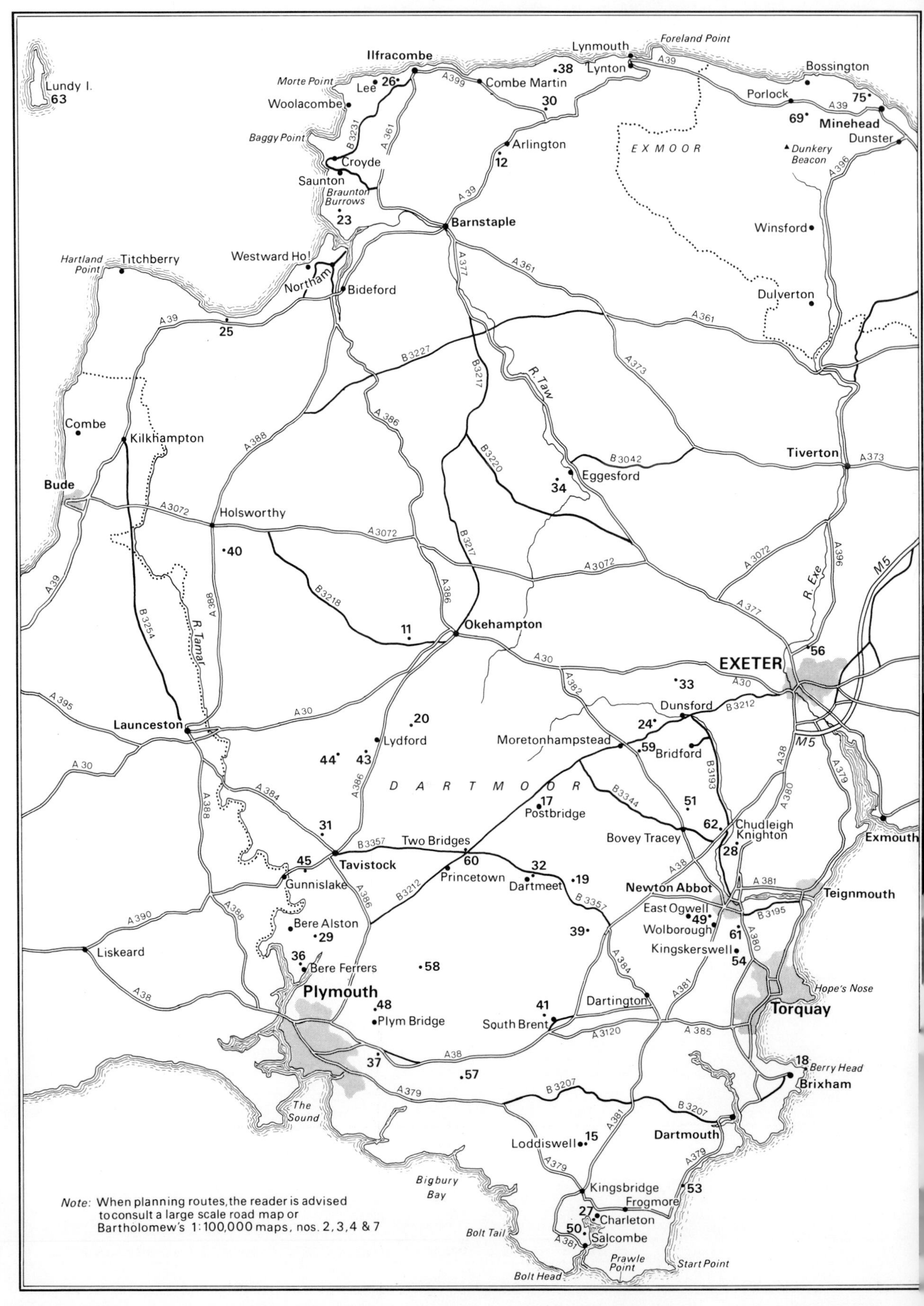

Lundy I.
63
Morte Point
Lee
26
Ilfracombe
Woolacombe
Baggy Point
B 3231
A 361
Croyde
Saunton
Braunton Burrows
23
A 399
Combe Martin
38
Lynmouth
Lynton
Foreland Point
A 39
30
Arlington
12
A 39
Barnstaple
E X M O O R
Bossington
Porlock
75
A 39
69
Minehead
Dunster
Dunkery Beacon
A 396
Winsford
Hartland Point
Titchberry
Westward Ho!
Northam
Bideford
A 377
A 361
Dulverton
A 39
25
A 361
B 3227
B 3217
R. Taw
A 373
A 386
A 388
Combe
Kilkhampton
B 3220
B 3042
Tiverton
A 373
Bude
Eggesford
34
A 3072
Holsworthy
A 3072
•40
A 3072
A 3072
A 39
B 3217
A 396
R. Exe
M5
A 386
B 3218
A 388
R. Tamar
B 3254
A 377
11
Okehampton
56
A 30
EXETER
A 382
33
A 30
A 395
A 30
Dunsford
B 3212
Launceston
20
24
Lydford
Moretonhampstead
59
Bridford
M5
A 30
44
43
B 3193
A 38
A 380
A 379
A 384
A 386
D A R T M O O R
17
Postbridge
B 3344
51
A 388
31
62
Chudleigh
Knighton
Bovey Tracey
B 3357
Two Bridges
28
Exmouth
45
Tavistock
60
32
Gunnislake
Princetown
Dartmeet
19
A 38
Newton Abbot
A 381
Teignmouth
A 386
B 3212
B 3357
A 388
East Ogwell
49
B 3195
A 390
Bere Alston
29
39
Wolborough
61
A 380
Liskeard
36
Kingskerswell
54
Bere Ferrers
58
A 384
Plymouth
48
Plym Bridge
41
Dartington
A 381
Hope's Nose
A 38
South Brent
Torquay
A 3120
A 385
37
A 38
18
Berry Head
57
Brixham
A 379
B 3207
B 3207
The Sound
A 381
Loddiswell
15
Dartmouth
A 379
A 379
Bigbury Bay
Kingsbridge
53
Frogmore
27
Charleton
Bolt Tail
50
Salcombe
A 381
Prawle Point
Start Point
Bolt Head
Note: When planning routes, the reader is advised to consult a large scale road map or Bartholomew's 1:100,000 maps, nos. 2, 3, 4 & 7

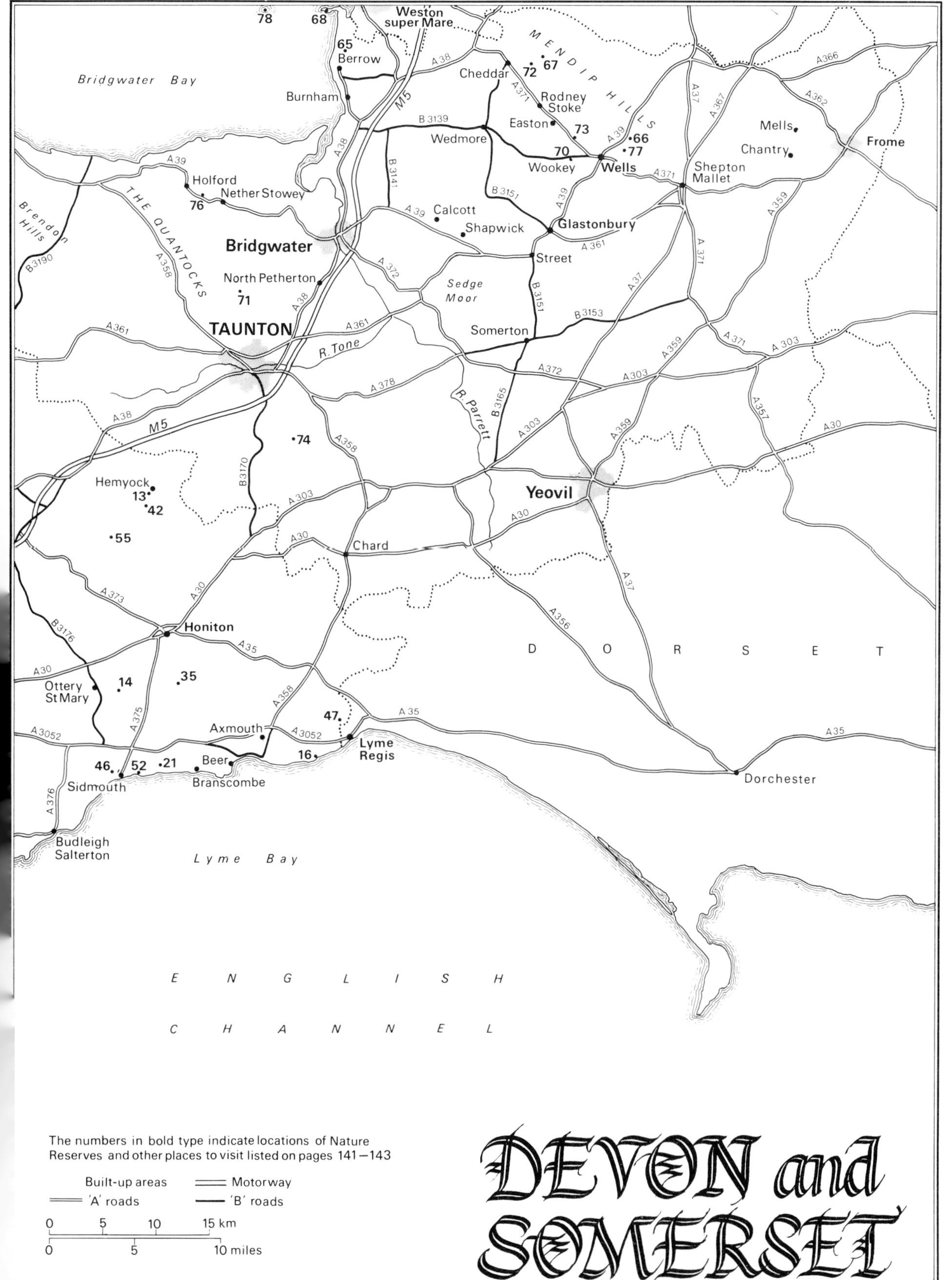

DEVON and SOMERSET

Some useful addresses

It is always helpful to voluntary societies if a stamped and addressed envelope is enclosed with all enquiries.

Bristol Naturalists' Society:
3 Ridgewood, Knoll Hill, Bristol 9, Avon.
British Butterfly Conservation Society:
Tudor House, Quorn, Leicestershire LE12 8AD.
British Deer Society:
Riverside House, Heytesbury, Warminster, Wiltshire BA12 0HF.
South-west England Branch:
Long Meadow House, Dunsford, Exeter, Devon.
British Naturalists' Association:
Willowfield, Boyneswood Road, Four Marks, Alton, Hants (local branches in West Country).
Camborne–Redruth Natural History Society: 57 Edward Street, Tuckingmill, Camborne, Cornwall.
Cornwall Bird-watching and Preservation Society: Lewidden, Penrose, St Ervan, Wadebridge, Cornwall.
Cornwall Naturalists' Trust:
Trendrine, Zennor, St Ives, Cornwall TR26 3BW.
Countryside Commission:
John Dower House, Crescent Place, Cheltenham, Glos GL50 3RA.
South-West Regional Office:
Bridge House, Sion Place, Clifton Down, Bristol BS8 4AS.
Dartmoor National Park Committee:
County Hall, Topsham Road, Exeter, Devon EX2 4QA.
Dartmoor Preservation Association:
4 Oxford Gardens, Mannamead, Plymouth, Devon PL3 4SF.
Devon Biological Field Databank:
Natural History Department, Royal Albert Memorial Museum, Queen Street, Exeter, Devon.
Devon Bird-watching and Preservation Society: Uplands, Looseleigh Lane, Crownhill, Plymouth, Devon.
Devon Trust for Nature Conservation:
75 Queen Street, Exeter, Devon EX4 3RX.
Devonshire Association for the Advancement of Science, Literature and Art: 7 The Close, Exeter, Devon.
Exeter Natural History Society:
25 Spruce Park, Crediton, Devon EX17 3HH.
Exmoor National Park Authority:
Exmoor House, Dulverton, Somerset TA22 9HL.
Exmoor Natural History Society:
26 Alcombe Road, Minehead, Somerset.
Exmoor Society:
Parish Rooms, Dulverton, Somerset 22A 9DP.
Field Studies Council (Courses in natural history):
Information Office: Preston Montford, Montford Bridge, Shrewsbury, Salop SY4 1HW.
The Leonard Wills Field Centre: Nettlecombe Court, Williton, Taunton, Somerset TA4 4HT.
Slapton Ley Field Centre: Slapton, Kingsbridge, Devon TQ7 2QP.
Forestry Commission:
S.W.(E) Conservancy, Flowers Hill, Brislington, Bristol, Avon BS4 5JY.
Holsworthy Natural History Society:
Thorne Farm, Holsworthy, Devon.
Ilfracombe Natural History and Field Society: 2 Bath Place, Ilfracombe, Devon.
Institute of Cornish Studies:
Trevenson House, Pool, Redruth, Cornwall TR15 3RE.
Kenneth Allsop Memorial Trust:
Knock-na-cre, Milborne Port, Sherborne, Dorset DT9 5HJ.
Lizard Field Studies Club:
Wheal Crease, The Lizard, Helston, Cornwall TR12 7NX.
Lundy Field Society:
17 Furzefield Road, Reigate, Surrey RH2 7HG.
Mid-Somerset Naturalists' Society:
Tamarisk, Gaunts Road, Pawlett, Bridgwater, Somerset.
National Trust:
42 Queen Anne's Gate, London SW1H 9AS.
Devon and Cornwall Information Office: Saltram, Plympton, Plymouth, Devon PL7 3UH.
Somerset Information Office: Stourhead, Stourton, Warminster, Wilts.
Nature Conservancy Council:
H.Q. for Great Britain:
20 Belgrave Square, London SW1X 8PY.

H.Q. for England: Calthorpe House, Calthorpe Street, Banbury, Oxon OX16 8EX.
South-West Region: Roughmoor, Bishop's Hull, Taunton, Somerset TA1 5AA.
Sub-regional office (Devon and Cornwall): 49 Brook Street, Tavistock, Devon.
Otter Haven Project: Yew Tree Cottage, Chaffcombe, Chard, Somerset.
Plymouth and District Field Club: 31 Widey Lane, Crownhill, Plymouth, Devon PL6 5JS.
Royal Association for Disablement and Rehabilitation: 25 Mortimer Street, London W1.
Royal Institution of Cornwall: County Museum, Truro, Cornwall.
Royal Society for the Protection of Birds: The Lodge, Sandy, Bedfordshire, SG19 2DL.
South-west England Office: 10 Richmond Road, Exeter, Devon.
Shepton Mallet Natural History Society: 8 Collett Avenue, Shepton Mallet, Somerset.
Somerset Archaeological and Natural History Society: Taunton Castle, Taunton, Somerset TA1 4AD.
Somerset Ornithological Society: Barnfield, Tower Hill Road, Crewkerne, Somerset.
Somerset Trust for Nature Conservation: Fyne Court, Broomfield, Bridgwater, Somerset TA5 2EQ.
South-West Water Authority: Information Officer, Directorate of Fisheries and Recreation, 3–5 Barnfield Road, Exeter, Devon EX1 1RE.
South Western Naturalists' Union: Shorton Manor, Shorton, Paignton, Devon.
Spastics Society: Churchtown Farm Field Studies Centre, Lanlivery, Bodmin, Cornwall. (Residential natural history courses for both disabled adults and children.)
Teign Naturalists' Field Club: Coombe Edge, 2a Woodlands Close, Lower Brimley, Teignmouth, Devon.
Topsham and District Birdwatching and Naturalists' Society: 10 Grove Hill, Topsham, Exeter, Devon EX3 0EG.
Torquay Natural History Society: The Museum, 529 Babbacombe Road, Torquay, Devon.
Water Space Amenity Commission: 1 Queen Anne's Gate, London SW1H 9BT.
Wells Natural History and Archaeological Society: The Museum, Wells, Somerset.
Wessex Water Authority: Somerset Rivers Division, Bridgwater House, P.O. Box 9, King's Square, Bridgwater, Somerset.
Woodland Trust: Butterbrook, Harford, Ivybridge, Devon PL21 0JQ.
Yeovil and District Natural History Society: Sunnyside, East Street, Crewkerne, Somerset.

Bibliography

SUB-REGIONS AND RESERVES

Allen, N. V. (1974). *The Exmoor Handbook and Gazetteer*. 3rd edn. The Exmoor Press, Dulverton.

Atthill, R. (ed.) (1977). *Mendip: a new study*. David & Charles, Newton Abbot.

Barlow, F. (ed.) (1969). *Exeter and its region*. Exeter University.

Bere, R. M. (1970). *Wildlife in Cornwall*. Bradford Barton, Truro.

Burrows, R. (1971). *The naturalist in Devon and Cornwall*. David & Charles, Newton Abbot.

Chapman, A. H. (Comp.) *An access guide to the nature reserves of England, Scotland and Wales for the disabled*. Royal Assn for Disablement and Rehabilitation, London.

Cocks, J. V. Somers (Comp.) (1970). *The Dartmoor bibliography (non-fiction)*. (1974). *Supplement*. Dartmoor Pres. Assn.

Coleman-Cooke, J. (ed.) (1970). *Exmoor (National Park Guide)*. H.M.S.O., London.

Cornwall Tourist Board. *Cornwall Coast Path*. Cornwall County Council, Truro.

Countryside Commission. Leaflets on the South-West Peninsula Coast Path.

Dartmoor National Park Committee. Leaflets: Outline of the geology (Dartmoor), Suggested walks, An in-print bibliography of books and maps.

Devon Tourism Office. Leaflets: A naturalist in Devon, Walking in Devon. Devon County Council, Exeter.

Devon Trust for Nature Conservation. Guides: Dunsford nature reserve, Salcombe Hill, Sidmouth.

Edmonds, E. A., McKeown, M. C. and Williams, M. (1969). *British Regional Geology: South-West England*. H.M.S.O., London.

Exmoor National Park Authority (1977). *Exmoor National Park Plan*. Leaflets/booklets: Outline of the geology, Suggested walks and bridleways, Waymarked walks, Cloutsham nature trail, Walks on North Hill, Minehead, North Hill nature trail, Minehead, Exmoor National Park Bibliography, Exmoor section: Somerset and north Devon coast path.

Forestry Commission. Guides to walks/forest trails: Bellever Forest; Cardinham Woods; Castle Neroche Forest; Coombe Valley; Deer Park Wood; Eggesford Forest; Halvana Forest; Halwill Forest; Plym Forest; Quantock Forest; Stoke Woods.

Gill, C. (ed.) (1970). *Dartmoor: a new study*. David & Charles, Newton Abbot.

Griffiths, A. and Bonham-Carter, V. (1972). The Exmoor Bibliography 1971. *The Exmoor Review* 13: 51–66.

Harvey, L. A. and Leger-Gordon, D. St. (1970). *Dartmoor*. 3rd edn. Collins, London.

Hoskins, W. G. (ed.) (1976). *Dartmoor* (National Park Guide). H.M.S.O., London.

Hunt, P. J., Wills, G. L. and Symmons, A. E. (Comp.) *Devon Wetlands*. County Planning Dept., Exeter.

Kenneth Allsop Memorial Trust (1977). *Steep Holm: mini-guide and map*.

Langham, A. and M. (1970). *Lundy*. David & Charles, Newton Abbot.

Lundy Field Society (1956). A bibliography of Lundy. *Annual Rep.* 10: 60; Additions. *Annual Rep.* 16: 34.

Mackenzie, P. Z. *The Isles of Scilly: nature trails and wildlife conservation*. F. E. Gibson, St. Mary's, Isles of Scilly.

National Trust (1978). *Properties of the National Trust*. Annual supplements in the booklet *Properties open*. Pamphlet: Country walks in Devon and Cornwall.

Nature Conservancy Council (1977). *The Somerset Wetlands Project: a consultation paper*. (1978). *Summary of responses to the consultation paper*.

Nature Conservancy Council. Leaflets: Axmouth–Lyme Regis Undercliffs NNR; Braunton Burrows NNR; Bridgwater Bay NNR; Dartmoor National Park and the Nature Conservancy Council; Ebbor Gorge NNR; Wistman's Wood Forest N.R.; Yarner Wood NNR.

Palmer, M. G. (ed.) (1946). *The Fauna and Flora of the Ilfracombe District of North Devon*. Exeter.

Pearce, A. E. Mc. R. (1971). A brief resumé of Mendip cave life. *Annual rep. Somerset Trust for Nat. Cons.* 7: 28–9.

Pyatt, E. C. (1976). *Cornwall Coast Path* (Guide-book). H.M.S.O., London.

Ratcliffe, D. A. (ed.) (1977). *A Nature Conservation Review*. 2 vols. Cambridge University Press.

Rouse, G. D. (1964). *The new forests of Dartmoor*. H.M.S.O., London.

Simmons, I. G. (ed.) (1964). *Dartmoor essays*. Devonshire Assn, Exeter.

Smith, C. E. D. Pamphlets: On and around Berrow Sand Dunes; On and around Brean Down. Somerset Trust for Nat. Cons., Broomfield.

Somerset Trust for Nat. Cons. and the Spaxton Society: The 'Quantock' series (pamphlets): Woodlands; Geology; Walks; Birds; Mammals; Plants. Leaflets/pamphlets: A Broomfield walk; A Quantock Forest Walk; Fyne Court, Broomfield: Guide to woodland walks; Black Rock nature trail; Longwood nature trail.

Storer, B. (1972). *Sedgemoor: its history and natural history*. David & Charles, Newton Abbot.

Turk, F. A. and S. M. (1976). *A handbook to the natural history of the Lizard Peninsula*. With *Supplement One: Flowering plants arranged by habitat*. University Dept of Extra Mural Studies, Exeter.

Wallace, T. J. (1976). *The Axmouth–Lyme Regis Undercliffs National Nature Reserve*. Serendip Books, Lyme Regis.

The Woodland Trust. Annual brochure (1978/79).

MAMMALS

(Anon.) *Discovering seals on the Cornish coast*. Booklet. Tor Mark Press, Truro.

(Anon.) (1975). Badgers and bovine tuberculosis. *News Letter* of Cornwall Nat. Trust 26.

Allen, K. (1975). Some aspects of the social behaviour of Lundy goats. *Ann. rep. Lundy Field Soc.* 25: 62.

Ansell, W. F. H. (1976). Information wanted on mammals and newts. *News Letter* of Cornwall Nat. Trust 27.

Bathe, G. M. and Scriven, N. J. (1975). The Japanese Sika deer of Lundy, with notes on the now extinct red and fallow deer populations. *Ann. rep. Lundy Field Soc.* 26: 19–27.

Burrows, R. (1975). Cornish mammals. *News Letter* of Cornwall Nat. Trust 26.

Chanin, P. Otters. In *Devon Wetlands*, 73–6. (See Hunt, P. J. *et al.* in section A of bibliography.)

Clark, N. A. (1977). The composition and behaviour of the grey seal colony of Lundy. *Ann. rep. Lundy Field Soc.* 28: 32–42.

Clark, R. J. (1970). Feral mink in south-west England. *Mammal Rev.* 1: 92.

Clarke, M. (1974). Deer distribution survey 1967–72. *Deer* 3: 279–82.

Corbet, G. B. (1971). Provisional distribution maps of British mammals. *Mammal Rev.* 1: 95–142.

Corbet, G. B. and Southern, H. N. (ed.) (1977). *The Handbook of British Mammals*. 2nd edn. Blackwell Scientific Publications, Oxford.

Corke, D. (1977). The distribution of *Apodemus flavicollis* in Britain. *Mammal Rev.* 7: 123–30.

Glue, D. E. (1970). Avian predator pellet analysis and the mammalogist. *Mammal Rev.* 1: 53–62.

Glue, D. E. (1975). Harvest mice as barn owl prey in the British Isles. *Mammal Rev.* 5: 9–12.

Harris, S. and Symes, R. G. (1975). The harvest mouse in the Bristol area. *Proc. Bristol Nat. Soc.* 34: 63–72.

Hooper, J. H. D. and W. M. (1965). Habits and movements of cave-dwelling bats in Devonshire. *J. Zool. Lond.* 127: 1–26.

Hurrell, H. G. (1966). The changing fauna of Devon. *Trans. Devonshire Assn.* 98.

Hurrell, H. G. (1971–2). Dartmoor badgers; Dartmoor foxes; Dartmoor rabbits; The small mammals of Dartmoor. Reprinted from *J. Devon Trust for Nat. Cons.* and available as pamphlets from Dartmoor National Park Dept.

Jackson, J. E. and Moore, J. (1976). The deer of north-west Somerset. *Deer* 3: 488–91.

Joint NCC–SPNC Otter Group (1977). *Otters 1977*. Nature Conservancy Council, London.

Lenton, E. and Webb, J. (1976). Otters on Sedgemoor. *Ann. rep. Somerset Trust for Nat. Cons.* 11: 28–31.

Lloyd, E. R. (1975). *The Wild Red Deer of Exmoor*. 2nd edn. The Exmoor Press, Dulverton.

Ministry of Agriculture, Fisheries and Food (1976). *Bovine tuberculosis in badgers*. 1st report (1977). 2nd report (1978). *Bovine tuberculosis in cattle and badgers*. Memorandum. Animal Health Division IIIA, Chessington.

Neal, E. G. (1966). The ecology of the badger in Somerset. *Proc. Som. Arch. & Nat. Hist. Soc.* 110: 17–23.

Neal, E. G. (1972). The badger in Somerset. *Ann. rep. Somerset Trust for Nat. Cons.* 8: 12–16.

Neal, E. G. (1972). The national badger survey. *Mammal Rev.* 2: 55–64.

Neal, E. G. *Quantock mammals*. Pamphlet. Somerset Trust for Nat. Cons., Broomfield.

Perrin, M. R. and Gurnell, J. (1971). Rats on Lundy. *Ann. rep. Lundy Field Soc.* 22: 35–40.

Rood, J. P. (1964). Studies on the ecology of the small mammals of the Isles of Scilly. Ph.D. thesis, University of Southampton.
Rood, J. P. (1965). Observations on population structure, reproduction and molt of the Scilly shrew. *J. Mammal.* 46: 426–33.
Rood, J. P. (1965). Observations on the home range and activity of the Scilly shrew. *Mammalia* 29: 507–16.
Rood, J. P. (1965). Observations on the life cycle and variations of the longtailed field mouse *Apodemus sylvaticus* in the Isles of Scilly and Cornwall. *J. Zool. Lond.* 147: 99–107.
Salter, H. B. (1974). Twenty years of 'myxo'. *J. Devon Trust for Nat. Cons.* 6: 11–13.
Spencer-Booth, Y. (1956). Shrews (*C. cassiteridum*) on the Scilly Isles. *J. Zool. Lond.* 126: 167–70.
Symes, R. G. (1977). Small mammals in Somerset. *Ann. rep. Somerset Trust for Nat. Cons.* 12: 21–3.
Turk, F. (1973). Distribution patterns of the mammalian fauna of Cornwall. *Cornish Studies* 1: 5–32.
Turk, F. A. and S. M. (1977). *Cornish biological records. Report No. 1.* Institute of Cornish Studies, Pool, Redruth.
Waterfield, M. R. (1974). Newnham Park Deer Sanctuary. *J. Devon Trust for Nat. Cons.* 6: 60–2.
Webb, J. B. (1975). Food of the Otter on the Somerset Levels. *J. Zool. Lond.* 177: 486–91.
Willett, J. A. (1975). Deer in Somerset. *Ann. rep. Somerset Trust for Nat. Cons.* 10: 12–16.

BIRDS

Allen, N. V. (1976). *The Birds of Exmoor.* 2nd rev. edn. The Exmoor Press, Dulverton.
Allen, N. V. (1976). *Bird life* (Exmoor National Park Information Sheet). Exmoor Nat. Park Authority, Dulverton.
Birds in Cornwall (annual). Cornwall Bird-watching and Pres. Soc.
Curry, D. A. *Birds of Plymouth.* City Museum and Art Gallery, Plymouth.
Darke, T. O. *The Cornish chough.* Bradford Barton, Truro.
Darke, T. O. *The Cornish sea bird.* Lodenek Press, Padstow.
Davis, P. E. (1954). *A list of the birds of Lundy.* Lundy Field Soc.
Devon Bird Report (annual). Devon Bird Watching and Pres. Soc.
Devon Birds (Quarterly). Devon Bird Watching and Pres. Soc.
Devon Bird Watching and Pres. Soc. Check lists: Birds of Devon; Birds of Dartmoor; Wildfowl and waders of the Exe estuary.
Isles of Scilly Bird Report (annual). Cornwall Bird-watching and Pres. Soc.
Jacoby, M. *Quantock birds* (pamphlet). Somerset Trust for Nat. Cons., Broomfield.
Lundy Field Society. Annual reports include comprehensive bird records.
Keylock, J. G. (1973). The bird communities of Great Breach Reserve. *Ann. rep. Somerset Trust for Nat. Cons.* 9: 21–3.
Lavington-Evans, C. J. (1971). Birds of the Quantock area. *Ann. rep. Somerset Trust for Nat. Cons.* 7: 22–4.
Moore, R. (1969). *The Birds of Devon.* David & Charles, Newton Abbot.
Moore, R. F. (1978). Some changes in the Devon avifauna 1928–1978. *Devon Birds* 31: 23–6.
Morley, J. V. (1976). Conservation of some Somerset birds. *Ann. rep. Somerset Trust for Nat. Cons.* 11: 17–19.
Palmer, E. M. and Ballance, D. K. (1968). *The Birds of Somerset.* Longmans, London.
Parsons, A. (1978). Bird ringing in Somerset. *Ann. rep. Somerset Trust for Nat. Cons.* 13: 17–18.
Penhallurick, R. D. (1969). *Birds of the Cornish coast, including the Isles of Scilly.* Bradford Barton, Truro.
Penhallurick, R. D. (1976). *A check-list of the birds of Cornwall and the Isles of Scilly.* Headland Publications, Penzance.
Penhallurick, R. D. (1978). Chiffchaffs wintering at sewage works in west Cornwall. *Devon Birds* 31: 36–9.
Penhallurick, R. D. (1978). *Birds of Cornwall and the Isles of Scilly.* Headland Publications, Penzance.
Penhallurick, R. D. *Birds of Cornwall: sea and shore.* Tor Mark Press, Truro.
Quick, H. M. (1964). *Birds of the Scilly Isles.* Bradford Barton, Truro.
Rabbitts, B. (1975). Birds of the reservoirs. *Ann. rep. Somerset Trust for Nat. Cons.* 10: 28–31.

Sharrock, J. T. R. (Comp.) (1976). *The Atlas of breeding birds in Britain and Ireland*. British Trust for Ornithology, Tring.

Sitters, H. P. (ed.) (1974). *Atlas of breeding birds in Devon*. Devon Bird-watching and Pres. Soc.

Somerset Birds (annual). Somerset Ornithological Soc.

Treleaven, R. B. (1977). *Peregrine: the private life of the peregrine falcon*. Headland Publications, Penzance.

Water Space Amenity Commission (1977). *Birdwatching at water supply reservoirs*. W.S.A.C. Information leaflet No. 4.

AMPHIBIANS AND REPTILES

Arnold, H. R. (ed.) (1973). *Provisional atlas of the amphibians and reptiles of the British Isles*. Biological Records Centre, Abbots Ripton.

Burton, J. (1975). Somerset amphibians and reptiles and their conservation. *Ann. rep. Somerset Trust for Nat. Cons.* 10: 23–7.

Gush, G. H. (1977). Amphibians and reptiles in Devon. *J. Devon Trust for Nat. Cons.* 8: 26–30.

Paton, P. (1977). Reptiles and amphibians. *News Letter* of Cornwall Nat. Trust 28: 3–4.

Wright, W. J. (1978). 1977 reptile and amphibian survey of Cornwall. *News Letter* of Cornwall Nat. Trust 29: 3.

BUTTERFLIES

Burton, J. (1971). Somerset butterflies and their conservation. *Ann. rep. Somerset Trust for Nat. Cons.* 7: 13–18.

Campbell, E. (1974). Butterflies in Cornwall. *News Letter* of Cornwall Nat. Trust 25: 3.

Comrie, J. K. and Neal, E. G. (1977). A Camberwell beauty in Somerset. *Newsletter* of Somerset Trust for Nat. Cons. 32: 6.

Cornwall Nat. Trust (1974). The large blue butterfly. *News Letter* 25: 1.

Fauna Preservation Society (1977). Rabbits, ants and the large blue butterfly. *Oryx* 14 (1).

Ford, E. B. (1945). *Butterflies*. Collins, London.

Ford, E. B. (1972). *Moths*. 3rd edn. Collins, London.

Higgins, L. G. and Riley, N. D. (1973). *A field guide to the butterflies of Britain and Europe*. 2nd edn. Collins, London.

Jenkyn, T. (1977). Devon butterflies. *Newsletter* of Devon Trust for Nat. Cons. April 1977: 11–13.

Sherwood, B. R. (1974). Outline survey of the Rhopalocera of Lundy. *Ann. rep. Lundy Field Soc.* 25: 70–3.

Skelton, M. J. and Heath, J. (1975). *Butterflies: provisional distribution maps*. Biological Records Centre, Abbots Ripton.

Smith, F. H. N. (1977). Lepidoptera in Cornwall 1976. *News Letter* of Cornwall Nat. Trust 28: 2.

Stidston, S. T. (1952). *A list of lepidoptera of Devon. Part I and Introduction*. Torquay Times & Devonshire Press, Torquay.

Sutton, R. D. and L. M. (1977). Evacuation of butterflies from Wimbleball (Exmoor) reservoir, Summer 1977. British Butterfly Cons. Soc. *News* 19: 11–12.

Thomas, J. A. (1974). The large blue butterfly. *Monks Wood Exp. Stn Rep. for 1972–73*, 71–2. Inst. of Terrestrial Ecology, Abbots Ripton.

Trebilcock, G. D. (1965). A guide to and local list of insects in north-west Cornwall. *Bull. Amat. Ent. Soc.* 268.

Turner, A. H. (1955). *Lepidoptera of Somerset*. Somerset Arch. & Nat. Hist. Soc. Records, Taunton.

TREES, SHRUBS AND OTHER PLANTS

Clapham, A. R., Tutin, T. G. and Warburg, E. F. (1973). *Excursion Flora of the British Isles*. 2nd edn. corrected. Cambridge University Press.

Davey, F. Hamilton (1909). *Flora of Cornwall* (including the Scilly Isles). (1922). Thurston, E. and Vigurs, C. C. *A supplement to F. H. Davey's Flora*. (1978). These publications reprinted, together with revised combined index, by EP Publishing, East Ardsley.

Giddens, C. *Flowers of Exmoor: a preliminary checklist of vascular plants (1974–6)*. Alcombe Bookshop, Minehead.

Hallam, A. D. and O. *Quantock plants* (booklet). Somerset Trust for Nat. Cons., Broomfield.

Hallam, D. (1976). *Exmoor National Park: Plant life* (leaflet). Exmoor Nat. Park Authority, Dulverton.

Hope-Simpson, J. F. (1975). Mendip rare plants in the context of their wider distribution. *Ann. rep. Somerset Trust for Nat. Cons.* 10: 17.

Hubbard, E. M. (1970). A survey of trees on Lundy. *Ann. rep. Lundy Field Society* 21: 14–79.
Hubbard, E. M. (1971). A contribution to the study of the Lundy flora. *Ann. rep. Lundy Field Society* 22: 13–24.
Lousley, J. E. (1971). *Flora of the Isles of Scilly*. David & Charles, Newton Abbot.
Marren, P. R. (1972). The Lundy rhododendrons. *Ann. rep. Lundy Field Soc.* 23: 46–51.
Murray, R. P. (1896). *The Flora of Somerset*. Barnicott & Pearce, Taunton. (1914). Marshall, E. S. *Supplement to the Flora of Somerset*. Som. Arch. & Nat. Hist. Soc. Records, Taunton.
Martin, W. Keble and Fraser, G. T. (1939). *Flora of Devon*. Buncle, Arbroath.
Miles, R. (1972). *The trees and woods of Exmoor*. The Exmoor Press, Dulverton.
Millman, M. *Quantock woodlands* (Booklet). Somerset Trust for Nat. Cons., Broomfield.
Paton, J. A. (1968). *Wild flowers in Cornwall and the Isles of Scilly*. Bradford Barton, Truro.
Paton, J. A. *Flowers of the Cornish coast*. Tor Mark Press, Truro.
Perring, F. H. and Walters, S. M. (eds.) (1976). *The Atlas of the British Flora*. 2nd rev. edn. EP Publishing, East Ardsley.
Sinclair, G. (1970). *The vegetation of Exmoor*. The Exmoor Press, Dulverton.
Storer, B. (1973). Succession on the Sedgemoor fens. *Ann. rep. Somerset Trust for Nat. Cons.* 9: 12–16.

Index

Figures in bold type denote pictures
This index should be used in conjunction with the lists on pp. 132–43

Abbreviations: FNR Forest Nature Reserve; NR Nature Reserve; NNR National Nature Reserve; SSSI Site of Special Scientific Interest.